UNDERSTANDING
TONY KUSHNER

Understanding Contemporary American Literature
Matthew J. Bruccoli, Series Editor

Volumes on

Edward Albee • Sherman Alexie • Nicholson Baker • John Barth
Donald Barthelme • The Beats • The Black Mountain Poets
Robert Bly • Raymond Carver • Fred Chappell
Chicano Literature • Contemporary American Drama
Contemporary American Horror Fiction
Contemporary American Literary Theory
Contemporary American Science Fiction, 1926–1970
Contemporary American Science Fiction, 1970–2000
Contemporary Chicana Literature • Robert Coover • James Dickey
E. L. Doctorow • Rita Dove • John Gardner • George Garrett
John Hawkes • Joseph Heller • Lillian Hellman • Beth Henley
John Irving • Randall Jarrell • Charles Johnson • Adrienne Kennedy
William Kennedy • Jack Kerouac • Jamaica Kincaid
Tony Kushner • Ursula K. Le Guin • Denise Levertov
Bernard Malamud • Bobbie Ann Mason • Jill McCorkle
Carson McCullers • W. S. Merwin • Arthur Miller
Toni Morrison's Fiction • Vladimir Nabokov • Gloria Naylor
Joyce Carol Oates • Tim O'Brien • Flannery O'Connor
Cynthia Ozick • Walker Percy • Katherine Anne Porter
Richard Powers • Reynolds Price • Annie Proulx
Thomas Pynchon • Theodore Roethke • Philip Roth
May Sarton • Hubert Selby, Jr. • Mary Lee Settle • Neil Simon
Isaac Bashevis Singer • Jane Smiley • Gary Snyder
William Stafford • Anne Tyler • Kurt Vonnegut
David Foster Wallace • Robert Penn Warren • James Welch
Eudora Welty • Tennessee Williams • August Wilson

UNDERSTANDING
TONY
KUSHNER

James Fisher

The University of South Carolina Press

Published by the University of South Carolina Press
Columbia, South Carolina 29208

www.sc.edu/uscpress

Manufactured in the United States of America

17 16 15 14 13 12 11 10 09 08   10 9 8 7 6 5 4 3 2 1

Library of Congress Cataloging-in-Publication Data

Fisher, James, 1950–
   Understanding Tony Kushner / James Fisher.
     p. cm. — (Understanding contemporary American literature)
   Includes bibliographical references (p.   ) and index.
   ISBN 978-1-57003-749-8 (alk. paper)
   1. Kushner, Tony—Criticism and interpretation. I. Title.
   PS3561.U778Z643 2008
   812'.54—dc22

                                                  2008006208

Contents

Series Editor's Preface

The volumes of *Understanding Contemporary American Literature* have been planned as guides or companions for students as well as good nonacademic readers. The editor and publisher perceive a need for these volumes because much of the influential contemporary literature makes special demands. Uninitiated readers encounter difficulty in approaching works that depart from the traditional forms and techniques of prose and poetry. Literature relies on conventions, but the conventions keep evolving; new writers form their own conventions—which in time may become familiar. Put simply, *UCAL* provides instruction in how to read certain contemporary writers—identifying and explicating their material, themes, use of language, point of view, structures, symbolism, and responses to experience.

The word *understanding* in the titles was deliberately chosen. Many willing readers lack an adequate understanding of how contemporary literature works; that is, what the author is attempting to express and the means by which it is conveyed. Although the criticism and analysis in the series have been aimed at a level of general accessibility, these introductory volumes are meant to be applied in conjunction with the works they cover. They do not provide a substitute for the works and authors they introduce, but rather prepare the reader for more profitable literary experiences.

M. J. B.

Acknowledgments

When Tony Kushner's epic *Angels in America* plays, *Millennium Approaches* and *Perestroika*, first appeared on the stage of New York's Walter Kerr Theatre in 1993–94, he wrote an article for the *New York Times* acknowledging his debt to family, friends, and collaborators who supported the long gestation period of the plays. In the same spirit, I wish to acknowledge many individuals and institutions whose support made completion of this project possible. Tony Kushner is first among them; his many personal kindnesses and his work heightened my passion for theater and for what the stage can contribute to understanding the past, negotiating the present, and imagining the future.

My new co-workers at the University of North Carolina at Greensboro indulged my distracted air while completing this book. While a member of the Wabash College faculty, a 2005 summer research intern, Braden Pemberton, was unfailingly good natured and effective, and Wabash students in three seminar courses on Kushner's plays between 1996 and 2006 raised engaging questions about the works examined in this volume. I am especially indebted to the following individuals for enduring friendship and support: Michael Abbott, Peter Frederick, David Garrett Izzo, Philip C. Kolin, Felicia Hardison Londré, Diane and Jamey Norton, Warren Rosenberg, and Tom Stokes, as well as departed friends, especially Erminie C. Leonardis, Lauren K. "Woody" Woods, Kenneth W. Kloth, John C. Swan, and Fredric Enenbach. I also appreciate the editorial guidance of series editor Matthew J. Bruccoli of the University of South Carolina and of James Denton of the University of South Carolina Press.

I am greatly indebted to my parents, Mae Hoffmann Fisher and the late Clarkson S. Fisher, and my three brothers, Dan,

Scott, and Biff. Above all, my beautiful and talented wife, Dana Warner Fisher, and our children, Daniel and Anna, are unfailingly loving and encouraging always, and anything I accomplish is by definition for them. Finally this book is dedicated to the memory of my grandmother Anna Shannon Hoffmann and her daughter and my mother, Mae Hoffmann Fisher.

CHAPTER 1

Understanding Tony Kushner

Tony Kushner's emergence as a dramatist began in the mid-1980s while he labored as a graduate student at New York University; although he was then working toward a master of fine arts degree in directing, his true passion was playwriting. Even before his school days ended, his plays were being produced, and he arrived on the cultural scene in a burst of critical approval and controversy when his *Angels in America* plays, *Millennium Approaches* and *Perestroika*, were first produced in San Francisco, Los Angeles, London, and finally on Broadway in the early 1990s. Kushner became one of the most talked-about dramatists of the era, inspiring favorable comparisons with titans of the American stage such as Eugene O'Neill, Tennessee Williams, Arthur Miller, and Edward Albee. Like them Kushner is a true innovator in dramatic form, and his work expresses deeply personal concerns, politics, and the cultural discontents of his time.

The range of Kushner's drama at the midpoint of his career suggests that his achievement places him among a select group of contemporary American dramatists. The diversity of his plays, the varied and complex themes examined in them, and the historical, literary, and political influences irradiating through them are singular. An "out" gay man, Kushner found in the aftermath of *Angels in America* that some critics were inclined to identify him as a "gay dramatist," while others, particularly Harold Bloom, describe him as a theological playwright on a quest for spiritual meaning in a postmodern world. On close

examination Kushner is both, but he may more precisely be identified as a "political dramatist," one for whom gay rights is a
central personal and political concern, and one for whom religion and questions of faith and spirit are critically important.
Above all Kushner is an activist, working beyond the malaise of
postmodern ambivalence to reinvigorate the progressive spirit
through a focus on not only the necessity for change but its
inevitability. Kushner's politics are leftist—he identifies himself a
socialist—but his political persuasions are linked to a humanis-
tic sensibility most fully exemplified by an iconic Kushner character, Prior Walter, the prophetic gay man dying of AIDS in
Angels in America. Abandoned and alone with his deepest, darkest fears, Prior rises up out of despair to move forward, even if
what lies before him is unknown and frightening; recognizing
that the preciousness of life is precariously bound to resilience,
to a willingness to face change and move forward, Prior is, in
essence, Kushner's dramatic alter ego. Intent on working for
change that, in his view, is the only way for justice, compassion,
and progress to occur, Kushner eschews labels and works from
a dramatic platform advocating progressive change and from an
inspirational foundation of knowledge drawn from his intellectual pursuits, politics, and private experiences.

Tony Kushner was born in New York City on 16 July 1956,
son of William and Sylvia (Deutscher) Kushner. Trained as musi-
cians, the senior Kushners moved their family, which includes
Kushner's sister, Leslie, and brother, Eric, to Lake Charles,
Louisiana. Kushner's father, first clarinetist of the New Orleans
Philharmonic, was a native of Lake Charles (his family owned a
business there) and had studied music at Juilliard. The Kushner
family home was filled with music, poetry and drama, and liberal politics. Sylvia Kushner, who was first bassoonist for the

New Orleans Philharmonic, acted in local theater productions, and young Tony was profoundly impressed by his mother's transformation into Linda Loman in Arthur Miller's *Death of a Salesman*. Kushner's parents encouraged his passion for masquerade and the illusory magic of the stage, and this serious child immersed himself in the vital inspirations of the great works of literature, history, and music.

Early in his adolescence, Kushner came to terms with his homosexuality; for a time he futilely sought a cure through therapy. He became the school radical "so I wouldn't be known as the school sissy,"[1] but slowly he came to accept his sexuality and acknowledged it to his family after moving to New York in 1974 to enter Columbia University. Kushner's "coming out" experience is to an extent recorded in *Angels in America* when Joe Pitt, a conservative Mormon lawyer, makes an agonized middle-of-the-night phone call confessing his sexual orientation to his mother. Joe's dilemma is never fully resolved in *Angels in America,* but in Kushner's case it led to his activism for gay rights and centrally influenced his writing and intellectual pursuits. Kushner completed a B.A. degree in English literature at Columbia in 1978 before immersing himself in the New York theater scene as a director and playwright. He found employment as a switchboard operator at the United Nations Plaza Hotel from 1979 to 1985, during which time he worked toward a master of fine arts degree at New York University's Tisch School of the Arts, which he completed in 1984. Trained as a director under the guidance of Bertolt Brecht–specialist Carl Weber, Kushner wrote plays for fellow students and found directorial opportunities.

Kushner began to demonstrate the breadth and virtuosity of his playwriting as early as 1982, and his range astonished critics, even those disinclined to appreciate his left-wing political proclivities. Kushner's dramatic output in this period includes *La Fin de la Baleine: An Opera for the Apocalypse* (1982), an early version of his adaptation of Goethe's *Stella* (1987), children's plays including *Yes Yes No No* (1985) and *The Protozoa Review* (1985), and one-act and full-length plays, among which *The Heavenly Theatre* (1986), *In Great Eliza's Golden Time* (1986), and *Hydriotaphia, or The Death of Dr. Browne* (1987) were most fully realized. In these Kushner explored themes and techniques evident in his drama ever since, and his early efforts brought awards and grants, including a fellowship from the National Endowment for the Arts in 1988.

Often compared with Clifford Odets and Arthur Miller, American dramatists with overtly liberal political sensibilities, Kushner is more truly an heir of European modernists Henrik Ibsen and George Bernard Shaw, although the most significant model for his drama is Bertolt Brecht, whose Marxism led him to depict the social realities faced by the disenfranchised expressed with antirealistic theatricality. Through his study of Brecht and an extended exploration of Marxist theory, Kushner came to view theater as inherently political and to see progressive change as both desirable and inevitable. His awakening in this regard was not abrupt but began in college through his readings of a series of leftist writers including Brecht, Walter Benjamin, and critic Ernst Fischer, whose *The Necessity of Art: A Marxist Approach* proved both disturbing and intriguing in its articulation of the essential social responsibility of artists. Fischer's notion that "art is necessary in order that man should be able to recognize and challenge the world. But art is also necessary by virtue of the magic inherent in it"[2] spurred Kushner to mesh the seemingly antithetical qualities of intellectual, politically committed, realistic drama with imaginative theatrical illusion. Most politically inclined playwrights in the United States, Odets and Miller central among them, adopted "kitchen sink" realism, although in *Death of a Salesman* and other plays Miller strained toward the lyrical realism Tennessee Williams introduced in the mid-1940s. While admiring aspects of both Williams's and Miller's accomplishments, Kushner was drawn to the episodic nature and antirealistic elements of Brecht's theater to achieve his own particular realization of Fischer's notion of theatrical "magic," which Kushner himself ultimately described as "the feathers, and the mirrors, and the smoke"[3] of stage illusion.

The Brechtian influence is evident in Kushner's earliest plays, blending with an original aesthetic style that increasingly became his own as he approached writing *Angels in America*. His encounter with Brecht's drama taught him that "within what is apparently a naturally occurring event lies a web of human labor and relationships. He teaches you to see that something can be the thing it's supposed to be, and not, at the same time. I got Marx, I think, through Brecht, and realized that the theater is astonishing in the way it presents that paradoxical sensation."[4] Mating politics with the emotionalism inherent in a lyric realism allied to that of Williams, Kushner sought to revitalize (and politicize) contemporary American theater, and in the process he influenced a generation of dramatists, including Suzan-Lori Parks, Craig Lucas, Naomi Wallace, and Richard Greenberg, among others.

Kushner's interest in Brecht led him to Walter Benjamin, most particularly Benjamin's "Theses on the Philosophy of History," a seminal essay for Kushner in crafting his approach to dramatizing history. Benjamin stresses that "there is no document of civilization which is not at the same time a document of barbarism," a barbarism explained differently as it moves from one teller (or "owner," as Benjamin says) to another; for the "historical materialist," Benjamin posits, the task is "to brush history against the grain."[5] The notion of brushing against the grain of history was understood by Kushner on multiple levels in the major plays he wrote in the decade between 1985 and 1995, most obviously in those works depicting historical personages or events. Sir Thomas Browne of *Hydriotaphia* or Roy Cohn and Ethel Rosenberg in *Angels in America* are obvious examples of such figures, although it is in fact the case that even the most fictional of Kushner's characters is caught up in the crosscurrents of complex historical moments. Kushner does not merely provide an alternative history; he presents it from an unfamiliar angle, whether it be from Browne's dank deathbed as he considers the acquisitive life Browne has led as capitalism took form or from mystical encounters between Cohn and Rosenberg, two adversarial figures from the divisive days of the 1940s and 1950s Communist witch hunts depicted in *Angels in America,* his "gay fantasia on national themes," as a defining moment in the evolution of American politics. This encounter, in Kushner's mind, encompasses the Reagan revolution, AIDS, and the intellectual precepts inherent in postmodernism.

Benjamin's assertion that one is "constantly looking back at the rubble of history"[6] became the guiding metaphor for the themes that flow through Kushner's plays. For Kushner it is the "most dangerous thing" to imagine a future that "isn't rooted in the bleakest, most terrifying idea of what's piled up behind you,"[7] and, although exuding a neosocialist doctrine cobbled together from his study of Brecht, Fischer, Benjamin, and also British Marxist critic Raymond Williams, among others, Kushner recognizes the potential for catastrophe resulting from the failure of theory. He overtly explores this notion in his pseudo-political vaudeville *Slavs! Thinking about the Longstanding Problems of Virtue and Happiness,* which seriocomically depicts the collapse of the Soviet Union's seventy-five-year socialist experiment and the resulting socioeconomic and ecological wreckage.

Kushner also found inspiration closer to home; among U.S. dramatists, Eugene O'Neill's most ambitious, experimental plays parallel the challenging dramatic goals Kushner set for himself. Kushner, who refers to O'Neill as the Promethean figure of American drama (and has written a screenplay about O'Neill), admires the two "strains" of O'Neill's plays, "a kind of personal drama and the epic drama, and I think I've been profoundly influenced by both strains."[8] These strains, in Kushner's estimation, "interestingly emerge in Miller and Williams. It's a sort of combination, because the plays of Miller and Williams are both epic and intensely personal and lyrical and non-epic at the same time."[9] The purveyors of American lyric realism, Williams paramount among them, set the stage for the group of dramatists slightly preceding Kushner, who in diverse ways reflect Williams and the two strains Kushner identifies in O'Neill. These writers, including John Guare, Maria Irene Fornes, Sam Shepard, David Mamet, and others, influenced Kushner, but the emotionalism, humor, and lyric language of Kushner's plays is most reminiscent of Williams, as are the phantasmagoric elements, which seem inspired in part by Williams in his most experimental vein (*Camino Real, Suddenly Last Summer*) and in part by magic realism from the literary realm. Kushner acknowledges that Williams "was an incredible early influence,"[10] as were a range of southern writers (Carson McCullers, William Faulkner, Flannery O'Connor); he says there is "a certain quality in my writing, a kind of purpleness in the prose that is definitely influenced by Tennessee [Williams] and by living in the South. I'm very glad I grew up there."[11]

Confluences of past and present are important to Kushner, both in the impact of earlier writers on his developing aesthetic and in those historical moments within which he locates his thematic concerns. Even those few Kushner works set in the present, such as *Homebody/Kabul,* reach back to ideas of the past through the imaginations of his characters and historical apparitions intruding on the action; in most Kushner works, which are set in either the recent or distant past, contemporary events are set against historical concerns. Literary influences provide Kushner with a range of stylistic and linguistic sources, and his broad knowledge of history enriches the questions at the heart of his drama. His politicized view of history sets in motion an activist spirit that imbues his plays. As a gay man, Kushner emerged on the American stage at a point of unparalleled crisis for the homosexual population; his view of the gay past and present in America led to *Angels in America,* his most acclaimed play to date. He found inspiration in the plays of such gay forerunners as Larry Kramer, Harvey Fierstein, Terrence McNally, and their generation, most of whom emerged after the 1960s to articulate the hidden lives of gays and to expose a "gay sensibility" that came to the fore in American drama in the work of Kushner and his generation as the AIDS pandemic began in the early 1980s. Along with the pioneering gay dramatists, later figures like Martin Sherman, William Hoffman, Richard Greenberg, and others focused on the individual and societal tragedies stemming from AIDS and the divisive debate over gay rights post-AIDS. Kushner aimed to historicize the gay experience in *Angels in America.*

The influence of the immediately preceding generation of gay playwrights on Kushner is essential to understanding his work, although the conflicted tensions within Williams's view of homosexuality, as well as the aforementioned influence of his lyric realism, most significantly influenced Kushner in the shaping of *Angels in America*. Williams's depiction of gay life in a deeply closeted era, his liberation of a gay literary sensibility, and his abiding interest in the tensions between sexuality and love in all forms are all facets of his work embedded in Kushner's consciousness. Critics view Kushner as a logical descendant of Williams, none more so than John Lahr, who writes that "not since Williams has a playwright announced his poetic vision with such authority on the Broadway stage. Kushner is the heir apparent to Williams's romantic theatrical heritage: he, too, has tricks in his pocket and things up his sleeve, and he gives the audience 'truth in the pleasant disguise of illusion.' And, also like Williams, Kushner has forged an original, impressionistic theatrical vocabulary to show us the heart of a new age."[12]

From Williams, Kushner also locates a model for merging tragic and absurdly comic elements, the complexity of fully dimensional, larger-than-life characters, and an emphasis on gender and sexuality. Issues of gender and sexuality are seen most particularly in *Angels in America,* the work in which Kushner most overtly focuses on homosexuality. Like characters in Williams's plays, Kushner's characters are often outside the realm of mainstream values, sometimes by choice, sometimes not. Prior Walter in *Angels in America,* the abandoned AIDS-infected gay man who must find strength within himself, is a central example. Prior learns that tolerance is not enough: activism is required. Although his own coming out was difficult, Kushner is devoid of the personal baggage from the closeted decades of the 1940s through 1960s that Williams struggled with; in fact Kushner, like other activist gay writers, is inclined either to demand equality or to assume it exists without asking.

As Kushner began his theatrical work, the AIDS pandemic added to the ostracism homosexuals traditionally faced within American society, and the tension resulting from this presented an opportunity for activism for full social equality. The sexuality of Kushner's gay characters is set against the myriad problems of life; homosexuals, he suggests, have the same problems of survival encountered by all, but they are faced with another set of problems within a society historically hostile toward gays. Their individual trials and tribulations, flaws, and strengths are tested by the culture in which they live, while the immediate horrors of AIDS and the tidal wave of history either carries them along or engulfs them. As past certitudes and the problems of the present shift beneath their feet, some characters are able to negotiate their way through and find their footing. Seriously ill, Prior, who sees himself as weak, even insignificant, proclaims at the end of *Millennium Approaches* that "I can handle pressure, I am a gay man and I am used to pressure, to trouble, I am tough and strong."[13] He has been severely tested by trouble, by pain, by loneliness, and by fear, yet these experiences yield up strength and clarity. Being "tough and strong" is Kushner's mantra for gayness at the millennium; active response leads past fear and oppression. Kushner calls for "pessimism of the intellect, optimism of the will"[14] in his activist approach to the dilemma of gays at the millennium, a notion carried through to the other minorities Kushner embodies as a Jew, a political liberal, an artist, and an intellectual. Mixing informed skepticism (pessimism of the intellect) with an activist spirit (optimism of the will) leads to progress or at least the hope of it.

In a sense Kushner is a microcosm of American minorities—gay, liberal, Jewish, and the product of emigrants from Eastern Europe; his status permits him to experience prejudice from many angles. Within this context the threat of AIDS, the political conflicts exacerbated by neoconservative and fundamentalist Christian attitudes that present AIDS as a punishment from a vengeful God, and the traditional oppression of gays lead him to consider the merits of traditional American values, particularly in the realms of politics and religion. As an ambivalent Jew, Kushner embraces that part of his ethnic heritage that has suffered across the span of human history, acknowledging parallels with the oppression of gays. He recognizes the "fantastically powerful homophobic tradition within Judaism,"[15] while at the same time being drawn to its traditions of spiritual inquiry. Kushner perceives connections between Judaism and homosexuality in that they share a history of "oppression and persecution [. . .] a sort of false possibility of a kind of an assimilation [. . .] as Hannah Arendt says, it's better to be a pariah than a parvenu. If you're hated by a social order, don't try and make friends with it. Identify yourself as other, and identify your determining characteristics as those characteristics which make you other and unliked and despised."[16] Being marginalized within a culture, finding identification through outsider status, which, in Kushner's case, comes from his gayness and Jewishness (not to mention his politics), is at the root of the perspective on history and culture found in his work.

One constant throughout Kushner's work is an obsession with loss. The devastating impact of AIDS became clear in the early 1980s as Kushner was commencing his playwriting career, and he experienced these losses within his community as well as loss in his personal life. His mother died of cancer while he was at work on *Perestroika,* the second *Angels in America* play, and his intellectual mentor, Kimberly Flynn, a close college friend he credits with assisting in the creation of *Angels in America*, was seriously injured in an auto accident that left her with lingering physical difficulties. These and other personal losses are set against those facing the homosexual community in *Angels in America* and are refracted through his distress as the American political landscape shifted sharply to the right in the 1980s. The Reagan administration's nonresponse to AIDS seemed to Kushner a catastrophic governmental failure spurred on by the rise of the Moral Majority and other organized political and religious forces, with tragedy as the result. Kushner calls for active resistance coupled with the realization that losses are inevitable and must be endured: "You can't conquer loss. You lose. To suggest otherwise would be to suggest a fantasy. . . . Life is about losing. Things are taken from you. People are taken from you. You have to face it."[17] Facing despair and resisting it to find hope and an activist spirit are central to Kushner as both a man and an artist.

Kushner's first important drama, *A Bright Room Called Day* (1985), equates the rise of Nazism in the early 1930s with the "Reagan revolution." The play failed to find favor, perhaps because its equation seemed too shocking, but with *Angels in America* Kushner tapped directly into America's deeply conflicted attitudes about homosexuality as the AIDS crisis took hold. As suggested by its appearance on various critics' lists, *Angels in America* has taken a canonical place beside the most iconic American dramas—Eugene O'Neill's *Long Day's Journey into Night*, Thornton Wilder's *Our Town*, Tennessee Williams's *A Streetcar Named Desire*, Arthur Miller's *Death of a Salesman*, and Edward Albee's *Who's Afraid of Virginia Woolf?* Like these works, *Angels in America* is an essential dramatic contribution to understanding the American character. As Kushner's style took full shape in *Angels in America,* he digested the many intellectual and creative inspirations on his work, leading critics to describe him as a revitalizing force—one responsible for renewing the political value of the stage and for extending its potential past lyric realism toward a bolder theatricalism, even as his plays also often seem to celebrate the traditions of mid-twentieth-century American drama.

By the mid-1990s, as acclaim for *Angels in America,* which included a Pulitzer Prize, mounted, Kushner articulated his belief that "since it's true that everything is political (though not exclusively so) it becomes meaningless to talk about political and nonpolitical theater, and more useful to speak of a theater that presents the world as it is, an interwoven web of the public and the private."[18] Merging public and private realms led Kushner back to Benjamin's "angel of history," an icon blown into the future by the winds of change, progressing inevitably while its gaze is fixed on the rubble of the past. This concept of the unstoppable sweep of history and the ebb and flow of change is evident in all of Kushner's plays (but particularly in *Angels in America*) in his focus on individual lives swept up in the maelstrom of social progress. The acclaim for *Angels in America* encouraged Kushner to map out a role for himself as a dramatist with a mission to challenge accepted wisdom while, at the same time, evaluating the past to discover what salvageable values resided in earlier political, religious, and cultural traditions. For Kushner the past may provide guidance through an understanding of the failures and successes of its values and traditions. Among this rubble, shards of knowledge may be located, providing knowledge for negotiating the unknown terrain of the future.

Kushner identified the Reagan era as an age of intellectual and moral regression, a period that established values that remain dominant in American politics and society. In depicting this, Kushner frames questions about a social climate of moral emptiness resulting from what his characters call a fundamental abandonment of a commitment to justice, community, and compassion by the political right as well as an abandonment of principles and the loss of the will to resist on the part of the political left. Reagan conservatism, coupled with the failure of 1960s-style liberalism to counter it, inevitably led the United States, in Kushner's view, along a decades-long course toward conservatism that continues today. Kushner fears a future shaped by the divisive red state–blue state bitterness of millennial American politics in which significant issues, from American foreign policy and the Iraq War to gay rights and economic justice, are reduced to a conservative-versus-liberal turf war. Kushner's politics are of the liberal variety, yet he seeks strategies above and beyond the political fray to guide America in dealing with the major social questions of the day to avoid the momentary and artificial political spin that he believes obscures reality.

Among recent dramatic efforts, Kushner's one-act play *Only We Who Guard the Mystery Shall Be Unhappy* (2003) uses the political moment to reflect on the meaning of contemporary events and national policies. The play assails the Bush administration over its decision to shift the war on terror from Afghanistan to Iraq, raising the issue of the "moral imperative" a country at war has "to think about the people with whom they are fighting and ask questions about them."[19] Advancing beyond hatred of a demonized enemy requires a positive approach, a commitment to the notion that moving beyond hostilities becomes possible only by humanizing that enemy. This theme is explored more deeply in Kushner's screenplay (coauthored with Eric Roth) for the Steven Spielberg–directed film *Munich* (2005), a meditation on the act of revenge by an Israeli-sponsored Mossad hit squad against those who planned the attack on Israeli athletes at the 1972 Olympic Games. For Kushner the long history of violence between Israelis and Palestinians can only be overcome through attempts by each side to humanize the other, which in the case of *Munich* meant a depiction of the Palestinian targets as fully dimensional individuals with families who, along with other innocents, suffer the impact of the violence. Similarly Kushner insists that the war in Iraq requires Americans to consider the human toll of the conflict. The vast cultural differences between the two cultures demand that Americans acquire a greater knowledge of the other culture; an emphasis on humanism, in Kushner's estimation, begins with a process of moving beyond conflict. Kushner invites his audience to apply his "optimism of the will" when encountering the racial, ethnic, or gender differences evident in the contemporary world with compassion and a willingness to create an equitable community of nations.

In the aftermath of *Angels in America,* Kushner was slow to release another major play. Instead he crafted some eliminated scenes from *Perestroika,* the second of the *Angels in America* plays, into *Slavs! Thinking about the Longstanding Problems of Virtue and Happiness* (1994). He also adapted several classics (*The Illusion,* his 1988 adaptation of Pierre Corneille's *L'illusion comique,* became a perennial of repertory theaters around the country by the time *Angels in America* opened) and wrote screenplays, beginning with the adaptation of *Angels in America* for the screen, which culminated in a six-hour television miniseries directed by Mike Nichols in 2003. In 2005 Kushner collaborated on *Munich* and worked on unproduced screenplays about a tax revolt, the state of contemporary education (inspired by a Brothers Grimm fairy tale), Eugene O'Neill, and Abraham Lincoln.

Kushner finally unveiled another major full-length play, *Homebody/Kabul,* in 2001; like *Angels in America,* it was a direct response to current events, in this case the rise of the Taliban in Afghanistan and what this rise portended for both the Middle East and the West. The play, initially written as a one-act monologue called *Homebody* in 1999 (and produced at London's Chelsea Theatre Centre) was later described by critics as prophetic, for as the full-length version began rehearsals for production at the New York Theatre Workshop in the fall of 2001, the tragic events of 9/11 took place. As a result Kushner's characteristic conflation of past and future met the present reality head on, causing some controversy and winning mostly appreciative reviews. Its insistence that, as fearful as it may seem, dangerous other cultures must be faced might well have been instructive under any circumstances, but in the aftermath of 9/11 and the ensuing war on terror that found its bloody expression in Iraq, *Homebody/Kabul* prophetically framed the questions facing America and its Western allies for the immediate future. In response to reporters wondering if the prescient play would go forth or be changed by the disturbing new realities after 9/11, Kushner insisted that, despite the suffering and mourning at hand, it was not a moment for silence from a society's artists and intellectuals.

Kushner's next major work, the libretto and lyrics for *Caroline, or Change* (2003), a drama set to music by Jeanine Tesori, met with positive reviews during a held-over run at New York's Public Theater before a four-month stay on Broadway. A considerable change of pace from *Homebody/Kabul, Caroline, or Change* saw Kushner's gaze shift inward to the personal costs of

America's racial divide by looking back forty years to Louisiana in this semiautobiographical work. *Caroline, or Change* probes the relationship of Noah, a little Jewish boy (and Kushner's dramatic alter ego), and his family's African American maid, Caroline Thibodeaux. Noah and Caroline have both suffered shattering personal losses and are dealing with deep confusions of faith, family, economics, and the hard realities of change, a word that takes on multiple meanings as a dispute over a twenty-dollar bill sets the play in motion. The change refers to money, but also the great social and personal changes faced by the characters, as well as philosophical notions of change and the painful processes of accepting what Kushner posits is its inevitability. The conflicts of race in America, the dynamics of family life, and the momentous social and political turmoil arising in 1963 (when the play is set) and what came after merged in a musical that some critics, including John Lahr, felt came closer than any other in the history of musical theater to creating a popular form of folk opera.

As *Caroline, or Change* took shape in April 2003, Kushner and his life partner, Mark Harris, editor at large of *Entertainment Weekly,* became the first gay couple whose commitment ceremony was acknowledged in the *New York Times.* Kushner's activism for gay rights continues in the new millennium, and as well as responding to diverse political developments, he speaks and writes on subjects of concern to him and that are reflected in his dramatic output. In the new millennium Kushner's plays demonstrate his continued experimentation with form and deal with an array of subjects, including the nature of love as experienced in diverse cultures from seventeenth-century France to the shtetlach of Eastern Europe, the rise of capitalism at the dawn of the Industrial Age, the moral dilemmas of the Holocaust, the failure of socialism in the Soviet Union, the troubled history and present of Afghanistan, the Iraq War, the environment, psychoanalysis, grassroots tax revolts, the relation of Eastern European immigrants to the formation of twentieth-century liberalism, AIDS, gay rights, the educational system in America, the relation of art to the individual spirit, religion, the meaning of loss and death, and the afterlife and ongoing relationships between the living and the dead.

Unlike many of his immediate predecessors and contemporaries among major American dramatists—writers such as Edward Albee, David Mamet, Terrence McNally, Sam Shepard, Paula Vogel, and John Patrick Shanley, most of whom might be described as minimalists in the themes and language of their plays—Kushner aims for an epic scope. Stretching the boundaries of American lyric realism with a voluptuousness of language and literary allusion, a mastery of history, complex and multilayered themes, and an imaginative theatricality, Kushner creates a viscerally and aurally appealing vehicle for the sociopolitical questions central to his plays. Few of Kushner's contemporaries are inclined toward more than a single topic of concern within a given play; Mamet, for example, may have explored the corrosive underbelly of capitalism in his most acclaimed plays, *American Buffalo* and *Glengarry Glen Ross,* but neither play offers the history behind capitalism's emergence nor posits alternatives. Similarly most contemporary gay playwrights focus on issues of topical importance to homosexuals while rarely expanding to a broader exploration of the historical, cultural, and personal spheres molding the character of American society and its relation to marginalized gay citizens. In short these dramatists describe what they see before them; Kushner chooses instead to stalk the corridors of history (and his own imagination) to search among its debris for fresh insights from which he can not only describe and weigh his time but imagine the unknowable future.

CHAPTER 2

Early Plays

A Bright Room Called Day and *Hydriotaphia, or The Death of Dr. Browne*

Tony Kushner began writing plays while still a student in the early 1980s, developing a style based in large measure on the seemingly antithetical inspirations of Brechtian epic theater and American lyric realism. As he absorbed these inspirations and their theoretical underpinnings, Kushner utilized key aspects of both to enhance his own wholly original style. The promise of a revitalized epic theater increasingly led Kushner to combine these earlier forms with his own postmodernist sensibility, which he understands as a merging of high and low popular culture and a stressing of the value of diversity, difference, and discontinuity, all intended to create what might be described as dramatic historiography, viewing cultural evolution through the prism of his political activism and outsider status as a gay man, a Jew, and a neosocialist.

Hydriotaphia, or The Death of Dr. Browne (1987; revised 1998) and *A Bright Room Called Day* (1985) were the first of Kushner's plays to exhibit fully these influences on his style. The latter provided Kushner with his first major New York production, in 1991 at the Public Theater; while the former was produced at New York University in its initial run and not staged again until 1998 when Kushner revised it for regional theater runs at Houston's Alley Theatre and California's Berkeley Repertory Theatre. "The moments in history that interest me the most are of transition,"[1] Kushner asserts, and both plays emphasize the effects of historical change on the conditions and individuals making the change and those living with the impact of those changes.

In the theatrical and intellectual phantasmagoria of *Hydriotaphia,* Kushner's dramatic canvas initially seems to be a small one. Set on the last day of the main character's life, *Hydriotaphia,* a fourteen-character farce with a morbid undercurrent, focuses on the meaning of that character's life to his immediate circle of family and friends and, more important, to his society at a unique historical moment. Sir Thomas Browne, (1605–1682), the play's protagonist and an historical figure, was a noted seventeenth-century scientist and writer fascinated by, among other things, the rituals of death. For Kushner, Browne is an exemplar of the rise of capitalism; in fact Browne is depicted as a seminal capitalist, and although his life reflects the superstitious times in which he lived, Browne becomes a primitive model of a modern-day corporate CEO. The play's social theorizing springs from this conceit, yet Kushner also explores the complexities of the absurd and existential experience of a human life. With *Hydriotaphia* Kushner truly commenced his career-long exploration of history, politics, spirituality, and gender, an exploration shaped by Brechtian techniques and the emotional potency inherent in American lyric realism.

Hydriotaphia is comparatively simple in its plot. Browne is surrounded by diverse characters, all seeking favor to win his vast fortune as he awaits death. Realistic and phantasmagoric elements are fused together in the character of Browne, who fears death (embodied as his brutal, unloving late father) and fights it, while his Soul (played as a separate character), prevented from ascending to heaven by Browne's refusal to die, longs for transcendence. The play has the qualities of an epic farce, especially in the vaudevillelike manner in which death, witches, and Browne's Soul roam the stage in an antic and chilling riff on the meaning of a life and the mysteries of death.

The actual Sir Thomas Browne was born in London, the son of a successful merchant. His first literary work, *Religio Medici* (c. 1635), written before Browne began practicing medicine in Norwich around 1637, was published in 1642 without his consent. It presents Browne as a premodern man of science who, despite being educated at Oxford, Montpelier, and Padua and his probing intellect, was still bound to the superstitions of his era. Three years after its publication, the Catholic Church prohibited the reading of *Religio Medici,* but other writers, including John Dryden, imitated its style. Browne's contemporaries compared him favorably with Shakespeare. Browne married Dorothy Mileham in 1641, and they had eleven children. In 1646 Browne completed his most ambitious work, *Pseudodoxia Epidemica (Vulgar Errors),* and it was followed in rapid succession by *The Garden of Cyrus, A Letter to a Friend,* and, in 1658 an essay, *Hydriotaphia (or Urn-Burial).* Browne was knighted by Charles II in 1671, and later Browne wrote two more works published posthumously, *Christian Morals,* regarded by some scholars as a continuation of *Religio Medici,* and *Certain Miscellany Tracts,* a work on a wide range of topics related to human and natural history.

Hydriotaphia is taken from the title of the 1658 Browne essay, in which Browne posits that God has not necessarily promised immortality to humankind. With this central theme as a starting point, Kushner depicts Browne as a grasping, emotionally barren conservative longing for some form of redemption or transcendence. Regretting his own sins but remaining unchanged—or unchangeable—in his attitudes, Browne is shocked to be experiencing the inherent sufferings of all humankind. In business with a stuttering pastor, Dogwater, whose motto "accumulate, accumulate"[2] is a mantra he shares, Browne has amassed a fortune. Exemplars of soulless profiteers, Browne and Dogwater have established a successful quarry by seizing Norfolk common lands and forcing off the resident peasants. As the quarry engines pound in the distance, Dogwater asserts that "God hates idle money as much as he hates idle men" (68), and Browne agrees while also mistrusting "a distinctly mercenary scent in the air" (167) as his partner and others vie for his fortune. Babbo, Browne's "imponderably old and faithful retainer" (76), halfheartedly tries to protect the dying Browne from an array of characters who are after his money: Maccabee, Browne's horny amanuensis, who wears a tin nose in place of the real one he has lost to syphilis; Doña Estrelita, equal parts Carmen Miranda, Charo, and Eva Peron, Browne's sometime mistress; Leonard Pumpkin, a gravedigger who seeks a way out of poverty through a relationship with Browne's unhappy wife, Dame Dorothy; Dr. Emil Schadenfreude, Browne's physician and resident fop, who expresses Kushner's fascination with life in death; Magdelina Vindicta, the Abbess of X, Browne's long-lost sister and a militantly subversive nun; three Ranters representing the homeless and afflicted. The machinations of this wild assortment of "real" characters are observed by Browne's Soul, an androgynous being who cannot ascend to heaven until Browne dies, and the grim figure of Death in the person of Browne's late unlamented father, who stalks him but is continually interrupted from ending Browne's life by the intrusion of others.

Among those interrupting are three Ranters, believers in an obscure seventeenth-century religion, who have come seeking revenge for the executions of women from their sect accused of witchcraft and convicted, in part, on Browne's testimony as an expert witness. Kushner explains that the historical Browne "merely stated that if we believe there is a God, we must concede the existence of Satan and of witches. He was not attempting to sway the outcome, but to his horror, the women were hanged. There was a sense of guilt that poisoned the remaining years of his life."[3] Kushner's avenging Ranters, like the witches in *Macbeth,* are kept on the periphery, adding a sinister quality and underscoring the primitive nature of Browne's scientific knowledge.

Much of the play's weirdly dark comedy emerges from Kushner's amusing amalgams of seventeenth-century stereotypes and modern-day counterparts. Unbridled Monty Pythonesque anarchy reigns and extends even to a crazy-quilt language Kushner concocts from a hodge-podge of Brooklynese, Teutonic, and Yiddish accents, with flourishes of Cajun and Creole. Mostly spoken by Babbo and Maccabee, this odd lingo is meant to mock the formalizing linguistic style resulting from straight British dialects and adds to the broad, cartoonish quality of the play's secondary characters. The language also adds a multicultural element, for this invented dialect liberates the play from particulars, and as such, the characters, with the possible exceptions of Browne and Dame Dorothy, become broadly drawn archetypes, and their world emerges as simultaneously familiar and strange. *Hydriotaphia*'s lunacy melts away, revealing a complex meditation on the power of death or, as Browne puts it, on the idea that "there's something vital and electric in morbidity."[4] About to become "worm food," Browne, observing the hypocritical maneuverings around him, understands Dogwater's statement that "Guh-God moves in mah-mysterious and sometimes ruh-rather malicious ways" (208), a comment reflecting the religious ambivalence pervading Kushner's plays. As darker tones emerge, Kushner locates a vein of Ben Jonson "humours" in his characters, each reflecting the mysterious and malevolent ways of humans as well as the God they imagined.

Kushner contemplates the forces at work in forging a human life. Browne, who was considered the equal of Shakespeare by his contemporaries and was an inspiration to writers (including Herman Melville), has, during intervening centuries, become a much less admired figure. In Browne's belief that God provides mankind no guarantee of immortality, Kushner finds a means to turn the idea back on its author, whose life exemplifies the social and moral tensions of an era. As a political dramatist, contemplation of death led Kushner, inevitably, to consider the ways in which society deals with death. In Reagan's America, Kushner believes, "a society that glorifies individuality at the expense of connectedness" and that "makes a virtue of isolation and pathologizes connectedness" leads its citizenry to "make our deaths hard. Death is terrifying because we fear extinction, find it inconceivable. America's obsession with youth is really an avoidance of aging and dying."[5] Describing *Hydriotaphia* as an "historical play only in the loosest and most irresponsible fashion," Kushner stresses its focus on death, immortality, and a society's "relationship to death: life and death, sex and death, money and death."[6]

Finding a political matrix even in a meditation on death, Kushner employs his historical figure to illuminate an era of transition. "I am interested in periods in history that seem to be transitional," Kushner says, those in which "an old social order is on its way out and new social orders are on their way in. These are very much representative of the period that I was born into—

that we live in now—a period of instability where we're turning some kind of a corner."[7] Such a time, he insists, offers possibilities that "range from a vastly improved world to no world at all. The big question right now I think is up for grabs, and I think that's been true for most of this century. And so I think I'm drawn to other periods in history where that was the case."[8] Browne lived during the early Restoration period, following Cromwell's rule and several revolutionary decades, a period that Kushner found similar to the 1990s: "Reaganism is to a certain extent a Restoration. Nixon began it: a certain resettling of the terms of the social contract along very conservative lines"; yet, at the same time, "the social revolution of the 1960s is still with us,"[9] smashing together two dominant social, economic, and moral tensions, unsettling the cultural order. In Browne's era Kushner finds "a particular time in the development of capitalism, the system we live under today. It's about how the political and economic system we live under affects everything, including the way we die."[10] The triumph of capitalism comes, in Kushner's vision, at the price of society's soul and conscience. The ways Browne has managed his acquisitive, loveless life, and his approaching death have a significant impact on the community around him, a fact that is of little concern to him. As the characters battle for his fortune, his only interest is a sporting one. His accomplishments as a scientist and writer offer no comfort, although Kushner notes that the play "also is about the death of a writer and the ramifications of his work"[11] (a subject Kushner returned to in his one-act play *Reverse Transcription,* which finds a group of playwrights illicitly burying one of their colleagues in an old cemetery). This last is significant, for Kushner the playwright was himself grappling with the power of the word, as well as the questions of what a writer leaves behind and the ways those works are interpreted by those who come after. There is a strong vein of gallows humor in *Hydriotaphia,* not unlike that in George Bernard Shaw's *Heartbreak House* and in other late modernist and postmodernist dramas, although in this case it is perhaps closer to anarchy à la the Marx Brothers. Kushner tempered the mixture of seriousness and farce in subsequent plays, but in *Hydriotaphia* it is front and center, clear in his mocking laugh at the fearful, unknown future (or lack of one) following death and the absurdity of attempting to comprehend the unknowable.

Critics identified a schism between *Hydriotaphia* and Kushner's later works, beginning with *Angels in America,* but on close examination the essential thematic terrain of his later plays takes shape in *Hydriotaphia.* The play's whimsical irreverence and its bawdy cartoonishness are both strengths and weaknesses; the antic nature of its farcical plot uneasily merges with the profundities of its themes. The overflowing thematic plate of this play, typical of Kushner, might well be considered a source of dramatic weakness in the sense that it becomes impossible to develop some ideas fully. Philosophizing about life and death, Kushner is facile in his depiction of the inevitable personal doom faced by every individual, finding both nobility and absurdity in existence and its end. To a great extent Kushner achieves this duality through his central character. Browne's mocking self-importance and insistent gravitas in the face of the rampant lunacy surrounding him takes on an absurdly comic air. Death is proving to him, despite his resistance, that he is of no greater or lesser significance than any other man. Browne's accumulated knowledge is useless, and his wealth, title, and prestige are meaningless in the face of the great unknown. Even his own Soul wants no part of him; it wishes to find its own expression separate from his corrupt values and rotting, bloated body. Kushner asks the question: are we victims of life and our mis- comprehension of the meaning of existence, or are we merely absurd participants in the alternating suffering and joy of mun- dane everyday life? Understandably he has no answer, but in imagining Browne's life and in the play's subtext of the anxieties of existence and death, Kushner raises the problem of what well- lived, moral life means.

The 1998 revision of *Hydriotaphia,* in which Kushner more sharply focuses the sociopolitical moral questions posed by the résumé of its central character, retains the play's unique combi- nation of farce and tragedy. Browne's self-centered greed and callousness toward his wife and friends is so total that it is outrageously comic, but Kushner is not without sympathy for Browne's lonely suffering while acknowledging his failings. "You . . . who must live through this . . . I pity you" (180), Browne declares from his deathbed. Dame Dorothy, who "can't bear the accumulation" (210) of her husband's life, is less senti- mental, believing her acquisitive generation to be "cursed by our gold," and she insists that Browne did not live an admirable life even if he "never meant to harm" (121). Browne's Soul shares Dame Dorothy's assessment and, watching Browne agonizing from a blockage that causes his stomach to bloat grotesquely, declares that his illness parallels his persona and that, as such, he "will die of constipation" (78). Once dead, Browne wishes to be alive again "to eat. To greedily engorge" (202) on the world itself; he is unrepentant in death, and as such, as for all those who devour the earth, there can be no redemption. Browne's world collapses at the moment of his death with the thunder of his quarry machines crashing into a pit. The pounding of the machines matches his final heartbeats, then all falls quiet as the machines and Browne tumble into a great abyss; for Kushner this is the only possible end for the machinery of greed and those greedy beings who own it.

For her part Dame Dorothy ruefully longs for "a thick skin" that "won't grow" (135) in order to survive the world her husband has created. She resolves to make the ocean crossing to a New (and perhaps better) World, one she imagines as a place of hope and compassion, a reflection of Kushner's guarded optimism. This New World—America—is, at the very least, a place where a fresh start is possible, although Kushner the historicist knows there is no escape from the knowledge that European brutality to Native Americans would bring Browne's ethos of greed to this New World. Dame Dorothy has no sense of this, for her America is an escape into hope, however fragile, that a better life is possible, that the lies, avarice, and spiritual corruption of the Old World may be left behind.

Hydriotaphia establishes Kushner's ambitions for a refreshed epic theater that, as he explains, explores the sociopolitical options of "a vastly improved world to no world at all"[12] through stage dialectics. Kushner acknowledged "a certain fascination" with death, finding it "sort of spooky and fun, but it's also an ancient and venerable tradition [. . .] I think ten years ago, during the [AIDS] epidemic, I had really started to come to terms with it. Clearly I think it influenced the writing of the play. It's sort of a gothic take on death and dying, and one of the fundamental principles of the gothic is that there's a kind of vitality in death which is, thematically at least, the end of all vitality."[13] Returning to work on the play over ten years after writing it was "weird," according to Kushner, because we "change in 10 years, so it's like something written by a different person."[14] He and the times had changed: "I feel more—how to characterize this?—

aware of being older, sadder, wiser. The world seems less explicit to me than it used to and somewhat more depressing. Contradictions accumulate."[15]

The accumulating contradictions were already fully evident in *A Bright Room Called Day,* which Kushner wrote in the same period but continued to revise toward its first production in 1985 and after, leading to its Public Theater production in 1991. In *A Bright Room Called Day,* Kushner again visits a period of historical transition, the year of Adolf Hitler's rise to power in Germany, to provide an intellectually probing drama relating the Nazi leader's ascension in the 1930s to that of Ronald Reagan in the 1980s. Combining a mostly realistic portrait of a group of German-Jewish filmmakers in Berlin in 1932–33 with the cultural anxieties of Zillah Katz, a motor-mouthed, Jewish, left-wing, feminist activist distraught to the point of madness over Reagan's dominance of American politics, Kushner uses a Brecht-inspired dialectical approach and divides the play into a series of episodes. These foreshadow the coming Holocaust and other post-1930s events as Kushner places the scenes in historical perspective via Zillah's reflections on the relationship of then and now. Invoking Judaic imagery—partly to create a mystical traditional past and the historical struggles of Jews and partly for humor—Kushner raises ideas of what is lost as one world, one culture, and one faith face extinction, concerns he subsequently investigated in S. Ansky's Yiddish theater classic, *A Dybbuk,* in his one-act *Notes on Akiba,* in *Angels in America,* and in other works. Kushner's religious ambivalence and particularly the rigid traditions of Judaism factor in many of his plays, yet his response is rife with as much affectionate longing as with challenging questions. In 2005 Kushner coauthored *Munich,* a screenplay that brought his ambivalence into full focus. Centered on the morality of vengeance (even when it seems most justified) and what happens to those individuals who employ violence in response to violence, *Munich* examines in a contemporary light the ancient Judaic notion of an eye for an eye and finds it an obstruction to true justice, an endeavor that only destroys the avenger.

A Bright Room Called Day exhibits the dark phosphorescence of Kushner's linguistic lyricism more lightly exploited in *Hydriotaphia* and is constructed in a cinematic style inspired, in part, by Brechtian episodic structure. Appropriate in this case, for *A Bright Room Called Day* depicts filmmakers and intellectuals in 1932 Berlin slowly coming to understand that the rapidly rising tsunami of Nazism is grim news. Kushner underscores their initial failure to recognize how bad things can get while the drifts of political and social conditions coalesce in the play. The characters cannot initially imagine much will come of the changes, but ultimately all realize that the unthinkable has become the normal state of affairs. Agnes Eggling, Kushner's protagonist, is a minor actress in German films who, along with colleagues and friends, lives a pleasantly bohemian existence. Watching helplessly as their country begins a frightening transition, each character arrives at an individual conclusion about strategies for survival, either by fleeing the country, resisting, or, in Agnes's case, becoming inert. She is an odd dramatic creation in that inertia seems an inherently counterdramatic posture (although Hamlet's malaise might offer a counter argument); in Kushner's hands, Agnes's indecision becomes compelling. She sees all that is going on around her and agonizes over the departures of her friends, who one by one recognize that to remain in Berlin means deprivation and very possibly arrest and death. Agnes's inability to move decisively in any direction leads to passivity, albeit that of an emotionally involved observer.

Kushner expands on Agnes's inertia by introducing theatricalizing elements. In the nightmare of Nazi Germany, Agnes faces her own particular nightmare—Die Alte, a specter of an old woman who once lived in Agnes's apartment and has presumably been dead for twenty years. Die Alte haunts the play, chanting an oft-repeated fairy-tale verse about the little penny man, a grotesque metaphor for Hitler. Agnes and her friends are also visited by Herr Swetts, "a dapper Devil out of Goethe by way of David Lynch,"[16] who confesses that his powers have been weakened in recent centuries but adds that he is finding renewed strength thanks to the multiple horrors of the twentieth century.

In early 1930s Germany, the social terrain is fertile for evil to grow; Kushner suggests that the rise of the penny man—or any murderous tyrant—may occur when opponents lack the resourcefulness or will to resist. The defeat of idealism (depicted by Kushner as the anti-Nazi Communist movement in which Agnes is peripherally involved) and the seeming demise of liberalism in post-1980 America become for Kushner the foundation for his controversial analogy of Hitler and Reagan. Some critics assailed Kushner as an opportunist, noting that when the play was produced in England, the equating of evils easily shifted to Hitler and Margaret Thatcher. Yet for Kushner the purpose of drama is its utility as a political instrument directed at the present moment. The literary facility of Kushner's work suggests his plays are meant to be fixed documents, but in his willingness to update and change plays, he owes something to left-wing Italian playwright and Nobel Prize–winner Dario Fo, whose "throwaway" farces are first and foremost intended as utilitarian political tools.

Kushner posits that if the horrific brutality of the Nazis represents a gold standard of evil, how is it possible to weigh other evils? For example, Kushner asks, could Reagan's moralizing posture in the face of the mounting AIDS pandemic compare with Hitler's massive organized executions? The Reagan administration's inaction, in Kushner's view, was evil, an act that was more than a mere sin of omission. If not equal to Hitler's atrocities, then how can it be understood? Zillah's absurd, lonely struggle against what Reagan represents is a strangely noble one to Kushner, who suggests it is all that may be possible in the face of overwhelming obstacles. In the final analysis, the ability to recognize evil and to unite in any form of resistance to it is all any individual can do. A lack of active resistance, in Kushner's mind, means the death of hope.

Kushner carries this further by the ironic juxtaposition of Agnes's world with Zillah's; both are living on the fringe of their societies, a perspective allowing them to observe the movement of their society away from them and what they believe. Kushner's emphasis in *A Bright Room Called Day,* as in most of his major works, is focused on how an individual survives being engulfed by the sweep of historical events. Kushner's juxtaposition of two eras allows him to view the earlier period through the filter of time, with an awareness of what comes in the decade following Hitler's rise to power, and to view the present in the context of the past. In short, tragedy becomes farce, as Kushner explains:

When we conjure up the past we run the risk of reawakening old nightmares, of being overwhelmed with horror. Conjuring the future is even more treacherous, because to attempt to envision the future we must resort to what is known, to the past, and if the past *as* past is nearly unbearable, how much more unbearable to look ahead and see only old nightmares staring back at us. Then again, considering the dire present, imagining that we have any future at all has got to be accounted a cause for celebration.[17]

The scenes of Agnes and friends represent the tragedy of history; Agnes's response to it drives her to adopt something of an intellectual and emotional fetal position. She can only freeze in place while Zillah attempts to act, although her actions are, as she recognizes herself, farcical. She rants against Reaganism, stressing that evil may come in unexpected guises, and wonders: Is evil an extreme thing? Is it obvious, or can it be banal, ordinary, and even comfortable? Reagan's grandfatherly media image, she suggests, may be a mask for something more malignant. Zillah's loony hate-mail campaign is obviously absurd, a ludicrous assault against the neoconservative juggernaut Reagan represents, yet she is compelled to wonder why anyone would regard a president of the United States as anything other than a moral reprobate.

Zillah also reflects on the past (through her consciousness of Agnes's world) and her own unhappy present, cautioning that her era requires "not caution or circumspection but moral exuberance. Overstatement is your friend: use it" (70). Her comparisons of Reagan to Hitler are intentionally outrageous, and she offers cautionary warnings, including one regarding the difficulty of getting a good night's sleep: "During times of reactionary backlash, the only people sleeping soundly are the guys who are giving the rest of us bad dreams. So eat something indigestible before you go to bed, and listen to your nightmares" (71). One of Zillah's comes from an old photo of a lone woman who is not returning the Nazi salute at a rally while all around her are doing so. Haunted by this woman, who could easily be Agnes, Zillah rants about the necessity of resistance in any form and what she believes Reagan's era portends for America. Simultaneously Agnes's life diminishes in episodes running through 1932 and 1933. Her continued inability to act as her friends flee, resist, or die leaves her with only immobility. Alone in a dark corner of her apartment, she is a trapped animal, and Zillah, restless with her own fears, expresses her response to Agnes: "She still can't sleep. Restless, like me. I'm calling to her: across a long dead time: to touch a dark place, to scare myself a little, to make contact with what moves in the night, fifty years after, with what's driven, every night, by the panic and the pain" (90).

A Bright Room Called Day is indebted to Christopher Isherwood's *I Am a Camera* ("I am not a camera," Zillah insists, "I am a zombie graduate student of the living dead" [157]) and Ariane Mnouchkine's *Mephisto* but might be described more appropriately as Orwellian agitprop. Kushner is above all a political dramatist wary of various forms of political seduction. Complete acquiescence to any belief system, political or religious, is a danger to Kushner, and the Nazi nightmare, the most horrific political seduction of modern times, becomes his means for expressing that danger. In this Agnes becomes Kushner's alter ego, for the persecution she witnesses would have been experienced by him on multiple levels had he lived in Nazi Germany, for homosexuals as well as Jews, political activists, and artists were all targets. On the other hand, Kushner is no Agnes. She succumbs to passivity, while Kushner chooses, and advocates, active resistance. In this Kushner's alter ego shifts to Zillah, the outraged, crazy exile from Reagan-Bush America (or Thatcher's England in the original British production). In equating the Republican revolution of the 1980s, reinvigorated briefly by

Newt Gingrich's "Contract with America," with George W. Bush's neoconservative era, Kushner calls for reengagement in political struggle. Ironic about finding leadership for resistance, Kushner has one of Agnes's friends say, "The age needed heroes. It got us instead" (67), but for her part, standing against the winds of what she regards as regressive politics that threaten to blow her away, Zillah (and Kushner) choose activism, even, and perhaps especially, when it seems most futile. Turning to the past for revelation, Zillah (and Kushner) seek knowledge sifting through its Benjaminian rubble. Lessons found may provide help for countering new evils, and hope may emerge to replace the inevitable despair.

Critics tended to find *A Bright Room Called Day* too despairing and decried Kushner's equating of Hitler and Reagan, while others had problems with the play's relentlessly grim tone, a view shared by *New York Times* critic David Richards, who considered *A Bright Room Called Day* "an ambitious, disturbing mess of a play."[18] Comparisons were made with the plays of British political dramatists Caryl Churchill and David Hare, and some reviewers praised Kushner's dramatic skills, particularly in regard to language. Linda Winer, writing in *Newsday,* approvingly described *A Bright Room Called Day* as "a big, dense play of ideas—a welcome rarity after an era of apolitical American isolationist theatre."[19] Kushner's usual phantasmagoric theatricalizing is present in the appearance of the Devil, the ghostly Die Alte, and in the intersection of two historical eras, as well as in flourishes of humor, but he is careful to avoid trivializing Hitler's evil and the tragedies of the Holocaust, which, although they are not directly depicted in the play, are inevitably present through a contemporary awareness of this most horrific outcome of Hitler's rule. Some critics felt Kushner's attempt to merge the

1930s and the 1980s was uneasily accomplished, while others discussed Kushner as representing the problem of the polemicist versus the artist, a tension critics often identify in political dramatists with the presumption that these roles are mutually exclusive. The presumed incompatibility between dialectical drama and imaginative theatricality has been consistent in responses to Kushner's work, as it was of previous political dramatists from Shaw and Odets to Hare and Churchill.

Despite the critical brickbats, *A Bright Room Called Day* has won greater appreciation in recent years. When Los Angeles's Theatre of NOTE produced the play in 2000, critics applauded "the intricate moral conundrums and layered theatricality,"[20] and subsequent productions, including a revival at Yale in late 2004, brought praise. As one critic noted, Zillah's rants were now directed at "a certain ex-frat boy" president and his aide, Karl Rove, who "may feel at home at one of Hitler's rallies."[21] *A Bright Room Called Day*, which seemed so focused on the Reagan era, proved more universal than its initial critics imagined through updated references. Reviewing the 1991 New York Public Theater production of *A Bright Room Called Day*, Roy Sander wrote in *Back Stage* that "time will tell whether Kushner will ever write a good play."[22] This question was answered in little more than a year when *Angels in America* began its Broadway run.

CHAPTER 3

Angels in America

Millennium Approaches and *Perestroika,* the two long plays making up Tony Kushner's *Angels in America,* are, in the manner of all of his major plays, explorations of the eternal cultural struggle between reactionary and progressive forces. In the case of *Angels in America,* his attention is focused on post–World War II American society—its conflicted values, its problems (and their origins), and its hopes. Kushner probes the ways in which the political poles of postwar conservatism and liberalism, changing sexual mores, and accepted belief systems have, for better or worse, shaped American life in the last decades of the twentieth century. The two *Angels in America* plays add up to an epic drama subtitled *A Gay Fantasia on National Themes;* in this, *Angels in America* bears a more than passing resemblance to George Bernard Shaw's *Heartbreak House,* a play coincidentally subtitled *A Fantasia in the Russian Manner on English Themes.* Shaw's play, also set in a time of turbulent transition, reflects the ways in which Victorian-Edwardian values are carried within the intellects and souls of diverse, emblematic characters residing in a confused present and facing an unknown future. Like *Heartbreak House, Angels in America* explores the confusions faced by a set of characters living in a rapidly changing social order. Their bewildered, pained existence is set against reactionary-progressive tensions of the late twentieth century.

In *Angels in America,* Kushner argues for a reevaluation of American society along the theoretical lines suggested by

Raymond Williams, whose 1985 essay "Walking Backwards into the Future" posited, among other things, the value of socialist theory in forming a society that places a higher value on community than individualism. For Williams and, by extension, Kushner, "thinking about the longstanding problems of virtue and happiness" necessitated consideration of the question of whether life was "an arena in which individuals should strive to improve their own conditions, or was it a network of human relationships in which people found everything of value in and through each other?"[1]

Laced throughout *Angels in America* is an insistent plea for a reexamination of cultural certitudes, particularly those in the arenas of politics, economic justice, religion, morality, and sex and gender. A reformed society, as Kushner sees it, must be built upon a progressive, humanist doctrine grounded in the hard lessons of history, a conception central to both Williams's theories and Kushner's *Angels in America*. For the characters in *Angels in America,* the anxieties of proceeding into an unknown future cause paralysis and considerable emotional suffering (as in *A Bright Room Called Day*), but over the course of the two plays a few characters ultimately conclude that stasis is more painful than taking the fearful journey forward. Walking backward into the future, as Williams articulates, is a means of facing the inevitability of change; by finding guideposts in past wisdom, the progressive traveler may avoid potential pitfalls. When Prior Walter, the pivotal emotional center of *Angels in America,* invites the audience to imagine progress that, in his case, translates to "more life,"[2] despite the ravages of AIDS and the emotional pain of abandonment he endures, he does so with his eyes firmly fixed on what lies behind him, on the stagnation of stasis. He accepts, and even embraces, the agonies of his life and, as such, achieves redemption born of a renewed hope, even if that hope is burnished with a knowledge that the joy of living is inextricably linked to loss and suffering. Insisting that no matter what humans are given to endure, belief in progressive change is a path to hope and salvation. Prior acknowledges that humans "live past hope" (136) and that a wary, battered optimism emerges from bearing terrible personal ordeals and from believing in an individual's power to change her or his own life, to find a community, and to contribute to constructing a better world.

In 1991 the first of the two *Angels in America* plays, *Millennium Approaches*—which Kushner had been working on for a few years prior—was produced at San Francisco's Eureka Theater under the direction of Oskar Eustis. The production moved to Los Angeles's Mark Taper Forum, and the play was subsequently produced at the National Theatre of Great Britain in 1992, winning the Olivier Award as best play among other kudos. *Millennium Approaches* debuted on Broadway at the Walter Kerr Theatre in 1993 under George C. Wolfe's direction, and Kushner was awarded the Pulitzer Prize for drama and the Tony Award for best play. Approximately six months after *Millennium Approaches* opened on Broadway, *Perestroika* also opened, joining *Millennium Approaches* in the repertory and also winning a Tony. Following the Broadway run and a national tour, *Angels in America* was frequently staged by regional and university theaters and in numerous international productions, occasionally accompanied by controversy.

The emotional and intellectual scope of *Angels in America* led critics to draw parallels with the classical dramas and with Shakespeare's plays, although it is rooted in modernist and postmodernist traditions of contemporary drama. Kushner casts his major characters into a vortex of past, present, and future values and questions; each character faces profound personal tragedy, ranging from abandonment and emotional despair to the collapse of the moral or religious certitudes that have guided his or her life. The possibility of death looms over the characters, who encounter each other and the dead. Kushner acknowledges the wrenching pain of enduring tragic circumstances, but he insists that tragedy teaches. The lessons taught are brutalizing and the losses suffered staggering and permanent, but in Kushner's world finding the ability to accept the inevitability of loss and change, and to progress, is a strategy for survival, both for the individual and for American society.

As a social progressive, Kushner's personal politics are paramount in *Angels in America;* he allows both political poles—conservative and liberal—to be seen and heard at their best and worst. His most conservative character, the historical figure Roy Cohn, does reprehensible things, but so does the play's most liberal character, the fictional Louis Ironson, who abandons his longtime companion in his hour of need. Cohn pays for his sins by suffering with AIDS, but the play's most sympathetic character, Prior Walter, also endures AIDS, while the play's most innocent character, Harper Pitt, must bear abandonment and the loss of the person she loves. Regardless of their politics or actions, each character faces overwhelming ordeals testing their beliefs and their ability to survive loss. Strong characters become weak, and those who consider themselves weak find unexpected strength within themselves. The survivors seen in the final scene of *Perestroika*, set in 1990, five years later than the rest of the action, have journeyed forth, carrying the lessons of their past—and the historical past—into a hopeful future.

Millennium Approaches begins in 1985 at the funeral of an elderly Jewish woman, Sarah Ironson, who is described by the presiding rabbi as an exemplar of the Eastern European immigrants who entered the American melting pot ("where nothing melted"[3]) in the late nineteenth century, carrying with them the rigid values of the Old World culture. "Pretty soon . . . all the old will be dead" (10), he intones, and with them go the experiences of assimilation, otherness, and oppression embedded within their lives that, Kushner posits, were guided by the black-and-white moral certainties they were raised to believe. The congregation at Sarah's funeral, made up of her grandson Louis's generation, has not shared these experiences and feels ambivalence about its own values. Louis and his generation see themselves as sinning against the firm truths of Sarah's world while navigating a grim, confused present and an unknown future without such moral certainty. In shedding the moral armor of the past, Louis and his peers are naked to the winds of change and can only look back, with longing, at those very values they have moved beyond, contemplating whether or not the resources needed to negotiate a rapidly changing society and personal travails can be found within themselves.

Kushnerian convergences of past, present, and future are deeply woven into the characters. Sarah Ironson as well as Prior's ghostly ancestors from medieval and Restoration England, victims of earlier plagues they equate with AIDS, are representatives of the past, as is another ghost, Ethel Rosenberg, who was executed as a Soviet spy by the United States in 1953. She haunts the play and her nemesis, Roy Cohn, as an icon of post–World War II fears and political conflicts. Three religions—Christianity, Judaism, and Mormonism—are seen as potent moral structures providing comfort and confusion to the characters, each of whom confronts the rigid certitudes of these ancient religious traditions. The historical circumstances depicted in the conservative mantras of Ronald Reagan's "Morning in America" are exemplified in their most hypocritical sense by Cohn, and in Kushner's assertion that Reagan's rise was, in itself, a demonstration of American society's loss of faith in community and compassion. Kushner's belief that Reagan represented a wrong turn for America, a view earlier expressed in *A Bright Room Called Day,* is reasserted in *Angels in America* through the characters of Joe and Louis. The unknowable future is represented in the plays by the notion that each character—and American society in general—must decide how to proceed into it, choosing between paralyzing fear or embracing progressive change, exemplified in *Millennium Approaches* by an Angel, who may be bringing news of salvation or apocalypse, and in *Perestroika* by the newly constituted circle of friends who have reconstructed their lives by accepting their losses, becoming agents for positive change, and by gaining wisdom through their suffering.

Angels in America is most often identified as a gay play, and it is indeed a reflection of reinvigorated homosexual activism of the early AIDS era, but Kushner moves beyond the political liberation of gays and the crisis of AIDS toward an exploration of the boundaries of gender (one of the play's conceits is that all of its characters are acted by a corps of eight actors, with men playing women and women playing men in some cases) and the complex intertwining of sex and love. In this Kushner is indebted to Tennessee Williams, a dramatist similarly concerned with the brutalizing realities of sexuality on fragile souls seeking love. Two generations of AIDS-era dramatists—Larry Kramer, William Hoffman, Harvey Fierstein, Terrence McNally, and Kushner, among others—present a range of views on the intersections of love and sex among homosexuals, but all were compelled to grapple with the death toll of AIDS and its impact on sexual politics. Few plays in any era garnered as much critical and editorial attention as *Angels in America* on stage and in its six-hour television film version in 2003, a fact suggesting that despite culture wars controversies, audiences found *Angels in America* to be a compelling framing of the political, moral, and sexual issues confronting Americans at the end of the twentieth century.

The intricacies of those issues, set against the tide of twentieth-century American history, confront the characters in *Angels in America* from its start. As the rabbi addresses the congregation in the first scene of *Millennium Approaches,* Kushner establishes an ominous mood describing Sarah Ironson's passing as a representation of the death of the modern American past. Chastising his listeners for ignoring the lessons of the past, the rabbi throws down a moral gauntlet as the two pivotal couples of *Angels in America* come to the fore. Sarah's grandson, Louis, and his lover, Prior, learn that Prior has AIDS, while a Mormon couple, Joe and Harper Pitt, recently arrived in New York, are in the process of confronting Joe's long-repressed homosexuality and the resulting implosion of their marriage.

In *Angels in America* politically conservative Joe finds a dangerous father figure in the rapacious lawyer-politico Cohn, who desires to make Joe his eyes and ears in the Justice Department in Washington. Much of *Angels in America,* particularly those scenes involving Roy and Joe, is set against the 1980s political and legal landscape; through them Kushner indicts American history, beginning with the white Christian majority that built modern America by stealing the continent from Native Americans through to the exploitation of slaves and immigrants such as Sarah Ironson. In acknowledging this past, Kushner also celebrates the framers of the Constitution for providing a legal structure that "very slowly and very painfully and at great cost" constructed "a body of laws, a tradition, precedence"[4] to protect ordinary citizens from unchecked ravages of capitalistic greed. Roy distorts the rule of law, but Kushner reveres its protections, even though they may be subverted.

Joe finds the possibility of Washington attractive, even if he does not know how to deal with his agoraphobic wife, Harper, who is addicted to Valium and emotionally dependent upon him. In perhaps the scene in which the diverse strands of the play's Brechtian (or cinematic) episodic structure and phantasmagoric qualities best come together, Harper, addled with antidepressants, and Prior, delirious from AIDS symptoms, meet in a hallucinatory dreamscape. Prior dons Norma Desmond drag to escape his deep depression as he experiences the frightening realities of his illness; this exhibition of a stereotypical camp sensibility is employed by Kushner as a mode of empowerment. Drag permits Prior an escape from his pain, while Kushner identifies in this masquerade a vein of broad humor that both plays on and rejects gay stereotypes. Harper's naiveté about homosexuals is set against Prior's camp sensibility. He recognizes that Harper is in denial regarding Joe's sexuality, while she sees in Prior a pure spirit; these two characters each provide clarity and healing for the other. When they later encounter each other in the real world in *Perestroika*, each is convinced they have met somewhere before.

Within the merged worlds of reality and fantasy, other revelations become possible. Harper confronts Joe about the repressed homosexual urges that nightly draw him to the Rambles in Central Park to observe gay men in anonymous sexual encounters. Joe, who has struggled to live by the values with which he was raised, explains his agonized battle to Harper: "Does it make any difference? That I might be one thing deep within, no matter how wrong or ugly that thing is, so long as I have fought, with everything I have, to kill it. What do you want from me, Harper? More than that? For God's sake, there's nothing left, I'm a shell. There's nothing left to kill. As long as my behavior is what I know it has to be. Decent. Correct. That alone in the eyes of God" (40). When Joe finally surrenders to his homosexuality, he phones his repressed Mormon mother, Hannah, in the middle of the night. In the scene, based on Kushner's own "coming out" experience, Joe confesses his secret to Hannah: "Mom. Momma. I'm a homosexual, Momma. Boy, did that come out awkward" (75). Liberated by this confession, Joe later meets Louis, who has abandoned Prior, now hospitalized as the complications of AIDS multiply. Disgusted with himself, Louis reflects on his behavior to the similarly faithless Joe, calling them "children of the new morning, criminal minds. Selfish and greedy and loveless and blind. Reagan's children" (74). Joe is not yet ready for an actual sexual encounter, so Louis turns to an anonymous encounter with a leather-clad stranger, who provocatively asks, "You been a bad boy?" to which Louis can only reply, "Very bad" (55). This scene frequently shocked audiences, although its most disturbing aspect results from its stark depiction of Louis's suicidal self-loathing (when a condom breaks, he insists that the stranger continue, not caring that he risks infection).

Louis's ambivalence mirrors Roy's self-loathing denial of his sexual nature. To Roy being homosexual means political weakness, and he sees himself as powerful—as such he cannot acknowledge himself as gay even when he is diagnosed with AIDS. As Kushner envisions him, Roy is a cynical and corrupt lawyer in the years following his infamy as Senator Joe McCarthy's right-hand man, juggling phone calls from angry, ripped-off clients and wishing he had eight arms with giant suckers, like an octopus. Kushner captures Roy's nature in his angry denial of his homosexuality: "Like all labels they tell you one thing and one thing only: where does an individual so identified fit in the food chain, in the pecking order? Not ideology, or sexual taste, but something much simpler: clout" (45). In Roy's deeply hypocritical opinion, fueled by his ultraconservative views, "Homosexuals are not men who sleep with other men. Homosexuals are men who in fifteen years of trying cannot get a pissant antidiscrimination bill through City Council. Homosexuals are men who know nobody and who nobody knows. Who have zero clout" (45). Kushner presents Roy as the very model of Reagan-era conservatism, which he portrays as adopting a trickle-down morality that has an impact on all of the characters, particularly Joe, who writes gay-bashing legal opinions as the clerk of a semisenile conservative judge. When Louis discovers this in *Perestroika,* he angrily confronts Joe and takes a physical beating as Joe lashes out in the only way he can deal with the evidence of his own hypocritical self-loathing. Kushner demonstrates a facility for merging the political and personal spheres in this and other key segments of *Angels in America.*

Kushner's conception of Roy as the symbol of bad faith at the top of the American power structure suggests that his corruption and hypocrisy ultimately infect society as a whole, as AIDS infects him. As such *Angels in America* presents a chronic societal disease, an ongoing moral combat represented at various points by the opposing poles of conservative and liberal, gay and straight, transgressor and victim. The cultural and personal struggles depicted expose complexities and contradictions within

American society and the individuals living in it. As Anne Fleche explains, Kushner writes "fantastically with one foot in the real, combining huge emotional and political stakes with a nonjudgmental, antisentimental approach."[5] Much of the tension comes from Kushner's balanced debate over opposing political forces and the overarching dynamic of his own leftist politics. Anger over the Reagan administration's resistance to dealing with the AIDS crisis and over the longer and ongoing struggle of gays for equal rights charges *Angels in America* with an intellectual and emotional force rare in contemporary drama.

Kushner's indictment of Roy's conservatism is paralleled by his similarly harsh view of traditional liberalism exemplified by the self-righteous and hypocritical Louis, who preaches liberal theory and compassion while selfishly abandoning Prior. There is no doubt that Kushner is sympathetic to fundamental tenets of American liberalism, and in Belize, a gay, African American drag queen, nurse, and caring friend to Prior, Kushner creates an activist who demands that theory become practice. Belize is Roy's nurse in *Perestroika*, as Roy's AIDS symptoms send him to the hospital. Belize condemns the failures of American society as represented by its government to respond to the challenges of AIDS. As he tells Louis in *Perestroika*, "I hate this country. It's just big ideas, and stories, and people dying, and people like you. The white cracker who wrote the national anthem knew what he was doing. He set the word 'free' to a note so high nobody can reach it" (96). Belize loathes Roy and everything he stands for, but he is no more sparing of the faithless Louis, whose liberal idealism is just "Big Ideas. Big Ideas are all you love" (96). Louis feels the sting of this and is guiltily drawn back to Prior, in part for forgiveness (or redemption), but although Prior will ultimately negotiate a new friendship with Louis, he makes it clear that they can never be more than friends. Disloyalty and betrayal of love are unforgivable crimes in Kushner's eyes.

Kushner emphasizes the value of secular humanism and belief in community in the attitudes of Belize, but they are also reflected in Prior, who lives with harrowing fears and profound loneliness. Cast out in a society of rugged individualists and moralizing politicians for whom he is, essentially, a nonperson, Prior's isolation is total. In *Millennium Approaches* he recounts the tale of an ancestor who escaped a sinking ship in a lifeboat with seventy other passengers. Whenever the lifeboat was about to capsize, crew members impassively tossed the nearest passenger into the sea. "I think about that story a lot now," Prior ruefully explains to Louis. "People in a boat, waiting, terrified, while implacable, unsmiling men, irresistibly strong, seize . . . maybe the person next to you, maybe you, and with no warning at all, with time only for a quick intake of air you are pitched into freezing, turbulent water and salt and darkness to drown" (42). In these fears Prior exemplifies the frightened inertia paralyzing Agnes in *A Bright Room Called Day,* but Prior, unlike Agnes, is able to conquer his fears. When an Angel crashes through the ceiling of his room in *Millennium Approaches,* he insists that "I can handle pressure, I am a gay man and I am used to pressure, to trouble, I am tough and strong and . . ." (117). Experiencing an explosive orgasm in the Angel's presence, Prior is awestruck as the Angel refers to Prior as a "prophet" and announces that "The Great Work begins" (119).

"The Great Work" to come may be interpreted in various ways, both in regard to what it suggests about society in general and for Prior as an individual. In *Perestroika* the Angel elicits Prior's support with a major problem facing celestial creatures: God has disappeared. He has not been heard from since the

1906 San Francisco earthquake, and although the angels are magnificent beings, they are unable to progress without his guidance. Kushner found inspiration for this in Walter Benjamin's description of a Paul Klee painting, *Angelus Novus,* which he sees as a figure about to move while contemplatively staring ahead. Benjamin writes that this "is how one pictures the angel of history," as a figure viewing history not as a series of happenings, but as a "single catastrophe which keeps piling wreckage upon wreckage [. . .] a storm is blowing from Paradise; it has got caught in his wings with such violence that the angel can no longer close them. This storm irresistibly propels him into the future to which his back is turned, while the pile of debris before him grows skyward. This storm is what we call progress."[6]

Benjamin's storm of progress blows through both parts of *Angels in America,* as the characters, caught up in historical changes beyond their control and by personal upheavals testing them, are challenged to the full extent of their emotional and physical endurance. Adrift in a time when past certitudes are crumbling, when the present is contentious and despairing, and when the future is a vast and fearful unknown, the characters experience a world that seems to be dying as a new, as-yet-unformed world is being born. In this Kushner strikes a parallel with the plays of Anton Chekhov or Tennessee Williams, for like the damaged souls of their plays, Kushner's characters have lost their footing. Tormented by the uncertainties of the future, their moral confusion, and feelings of inexplicable loss, Kushner's characters are rubbed raw; they are vulnerable beings adrift as the winds of change carry them to an unknown destination. This formula recurs in all of Kushner's major works, from early plays like *Hydriotaphia* and *A Bright Room Called Day* to post–*Angels in America* works such as *Slavs!, Homebody/Kabul,* and *Caroline, or Change.* In *Angels in America* Kushner establishes the unsettling circumstances when a nameless, homeless woman predicts that, in the new century, "I think we will all be insane" (105). Kushner situates his themes within such fears to imagine what lies ahead as old values are discarded as valueless. Without the moral guides of the past, his characters become intellectually and emotionally homeless, searching the wreckage of the past for clues. Kushner concludes that society must be remade, and although it may be rebuilt upon bricks from the rubble of the past, there is no governing blueprint or, in fact, much of a past, as Louis makes clear when he says, "There are no angels in America, no spiritual past, no racial past, there's only the political" (92).

The centrality of politics in *Angels in America* is most evident in the character of Roy Cohn, a behind-the-scenes politician who revels in his clout; there is no room for compassion in his brand of conservatism: power is all. When Joe confides the guilt he feels about leaving Harper, Cohn advises him to "learn at least this: What you are capable of. Let nothing stand in your way" (58). Louis, the play's liberal exemplar, has actually done what Cohn advises Joe to do. Unable to deal with Prior's illness, Louis walks away; he learns what he is capable of, and his remorse morphs into self-loathing. Cohn however does not judge himself harshly; he seems incapable of self-reflection or remorse. Near the end of *Millennium Approaches,* as he becomes delirious with AIDS symptoms, Cohn is haunted by Ethel Rosenberg's ghost. Proudly instrumental in sending her to the electric chair for treason years earlier through illegal ex parte communication with the trial judge, Cohn is unrepentant, boasting of having "*forced* my way into history. I ain't never gonna die." But Ethel warns him, "History is about to crack wide open. Millennium approaches" (112). Characters devastated by the realities unset-tling their lives in *Millennium Approaches* are compelled in *Per-estroika* to either perish with the past or journey into the future, and it becomes clear that the twentieth century—the American century—is fading into the mists of history; the individuals in *Angels in America,* and the society in which they live, must now reconsider their roles. Armed only with what they have learned from their personal crucibles and the past, the characters must choose a new path at the crossroads of a new millennium.

Kushner darkens the tone in *Perestroika*, but at least some of its characters offer hope, imagining redemption through the courage to abandon the cold comfort of familiar pain and outmoded beliefs, to cultivate forgiveness, to feel for fellow suf-ferers, and to develop a personal code of behavior based on com-passion and a will to function in a strange new world. This central thesis is developed through the ongoing experiences of the characters in numerous ways. Belize reluctantly nurses Cohn despite hateful taunts and threats, generously advising Cohn to exercise his political clout to acquire AZT, the breakthrough AIDS drug then in its test phase. Despite the potentially life-saving advice, Cohn continues to mistrust Belize, calling him "a butterfingers spook faggot nurse. I think . . . you have little rea-son to want to help me" (30). Indeed; however Belize, who bases his life on compassion, does not think like Cohn, wryly replying, "Consider it solidarity. One faggot to another" (30). Cohn gets AZT by threatening Reagan administration officials that he will tell what he knows (or guesses) lurks behind the Iran-Contra scandal. Cohn, who has been transformed, at least in his own mind, into one of the disenfranchised he bitterly disdains, explains his dilemma to Ethel: "Americans have no use for sick. Look at Reagan: He's so healthy he's hardly human, he's a hundred if he's a day, he takes a slug in his chest and two days later he's out west riding ponies in his PJ's. I mean who does that? That's America. It's just no country for the infirm" (62). But for Cohn this experience of disenfranchisement does nothing to increase his compassion for those in a similar dilemma, and he dies unrepentant.

Cohn is nevertheless the beneficiary of compassion from others. At the behest of Belize, Louis chants the Kaddish over Cohn's corpse (joined by the ghost of Ethel) in what Belize considers a fair trade for taking Cohn's stash of AZT, which he will use to help Prior and others. Even Cohn may be forgiven his transgressions, and as Belize makes clear, it is a blessing to forgive an enemy. Cohn and Belize are not the only unlikely pairing in *Perestroika,* for Kushner recognizes the possibility of expanding the moral and political debate and of exploiting and smashing long-standing stereotypes both sides hold by bringing together seeming opposites. Prior and Hannah, Joe's mother, become acquainted when she encounters him in physical distress and helps him to a hospital. Wary of each other, they slowly find common ground. Hannah, who has searched in vain for the errant Joe, learns about her son's struggle with homosexuality from Prior, while Prior simply needs a caring friend. Hannah may have lost her son as a result of the values she taught him, which are at odds with his true nature, but Prior teaches her tolerance and compassion for homosexuals. Leaving his hospital room, Hannah asks him if she should come again, and Prior, borrowing Tennessee Williams's famous line, says, "Please do. I have always depended on the kindness of strangers," to which the unaware Hannah can only reply, "Well that's a stupid thing to do" (141). Hannah does return and has her own encounter with Prior's Angel, inspiring an orgasmic liberation similar to the one he experienced in *Millennium Approaches*—and she is transformed by it.

Hannah also cares for Harper. Taking a job at New York's Mormon Welcome Center, Hannah brings the distraught Harper to work, where she sits all day watching a life-size diorama of a Mormon pioneer family crossing the Great Plains. Convinced she sees Joe in the image of the "Mormon Father," Harper pleads for guidance from the "Mormon Mother," and when the figure comes wondrously to life, Kushner achieves a transcendent meeting of past and present, which, like Harper's encounter with Prior in their mutual fever dream in *Millennium Approaches*, creates a unique space in which the mythologies of human history and literature converge with contemporary reality. The Mormon Mother's advice is hard, noting that loss and change rip one apart and that it remains for that individual to put herself back together. Harper is not comforted, but she begins the process of starting over. This underscores a central theme, that loss and the ability to live with loss—not succumbing to pain and wrenching changes that come with loss, whether the loss is personal or cultural—are essential. If *Millennium Approaches* depicts these losses while offering a glimpse of the retreating conscience of American society during the Reagan era, *Perestroika* finds its characters moving toward a reevaluation of themselves and their relationships and accepting the inevitable changes.

Kushner concludes *Angels in America* on a note of hope in a scene set at Central Park's Bethesda fountain. With a statue of a healing angel at its center, the fountain at the end of *Perestroika* symbolizes a final statement of hope, compassion, and forgiveness. Prior, Hannah, Belize, and a contrite Louis meet there as exemplars of a new American family. A wiser, more sophisticated

Hannah asserts Kushner's view of the interconnectedness of all humanity, regardless of race, sexual preference, religion, or politics and of the primacy of loyalty and commitment to others and to society. Prior points out the angel of the fountain, a figure commemorating death but suggesting "a world without dying" (147). Louis explains that the angel Bethesda "descended and just her foot touched earth. And where it did, a fountain shot up from the ground," as Belize adds that if "anyone who was suffering, in the body or the spirit, walked through the waters of the fountain of Bethesda, they would be healed, washed clean of pain" (147). Prior, the reluctant prophet returned from heaven where he delivered a plea for "more life" (148) and with his AIDS symptoms stabilized, claims that the healing waters of the fountain are not flowing at present but hopes one day it will heal again. In a final statement Prior offers a challenge that encapsulates his guarded optimism: "This disease will be the end of many of us, but not nearly all, and the dead will be commemorated and will struggle on with the living, and we are not going away. We won't die secret deaths anymore. The world only spins forward. We will be citizens. The time has come" (148).

Critics praised *Angels in America* as the best American drama in decades, a work comparable to Eugene O'Neill's *Long Day's Journey into Night,* Tennessee Williams's *A Streetcar Named Desire,* and Edward Albee's *Who's Afraid of Virginia Woolf?* Anna Quindlen, editorializing in the *New York Times,* called *Angels in America* "a brilliant, brilliant play about love and the human condition at a time when our understanding of what it means to be human and loving has, thankfully, expanded,"[7] while others probed the influences on Kushner, from Brecht to Williams. In interviews Kushner has spoken of writing additional *Angels in America* plays (most particularly one focusing on the Pitt family), and he did complete two smaller-scale works closely related to *Angels in America*.

The slighter of the two, a 1996 one-act play, *G. David Schine in Hell* (alternately titled *A Backstage Pass to Hell*), centers on Roy Cohn, who is residing in hell (as he does in a short scene in *Perestroika*), which, in Kushner's imagination, resembles a dinner theater in Orange County, California. The real Schine, who died in a single-engine plane crash in 1996, was himself an insignificant figure, yet he improbably acted as catalyst for the political fall of Cohn and, more important, Cohn's boss, Senator Joe McCarthy. Schine, who worked as a consultant for McCarthy before and during the Army-McCarthy hearings of 1953–54, became the center of a public storm when he was drafted. McCarthy and Cohn applied pressure on the military to obtain preferential treatment and a commission as an officer for Schine (reported by some historians to be Cohn's lover—or, at least, the object of his affection). The acrimonious Army-McCarthy hearings, intended to expose alleged Communist infiltration of the Army Communications Center at Fort Monmouth, New Jersey, came to an acrimonious climax when the army's lawyers revealed the manipulations of McCarthy's office to win Schine, who entered the army as a private, special treatment. Most damaging to McCarthy was the revelation of a doctored photo meant to enhance Schine's reputation by adding his image to a photograph of Secretary of the Army Robert T. Stevens. When McCarthy recklessly accused a young member of the staff of army lawyer Joseph Welch of Communist leanings, Welch angrily spoke the famous words, "Have you no decency, at long last, sir, have you no decency at all?" (110). Kushner revisits these words in *Perestroika* when Louis, confronting Joe with the evidence of his gay-bashing legal briefs, quotes them.

As *G. David Schine in Hell* begins, Schine sees Roy and realizes "This *must* be Hell!"[8] Roy explains to Schine that they are better off in hell, for heaven is "fulla kvetchy communists" discussing "why the Great Leap Forward turned into History's Biggest Bellyflop" (233). Hell, it seems, is full of Republicans, including homophobic North Carolina senator Jesse Helms, who, Cohn explains, is "not dead but he has a backstage pass" (233), and some Democrats. Schine, who is transformed into a handsome young man in a GI uniform, asks why Roy is not similarly transformed, to which Cohn replies that "as the very Embodiment or rather as the Spirit of American Conservatism, I *can't* change, it wouldn't look good" (234). Cohn is ecstatic to see Schine, describing their story as "epic, it's tragic, it's . . . *South Pacific,* Dave, my doomed love for you turned you into history" (235). Other iconic post–World War II figures appear, including Alger Hiss and Richard M. Nixon, fresh from "finishing my 75th volume of memoirs and geopolitical stratagems," who would prefer heaven "where people still believe in Government. I want some (expletive deleted) respect." J. Edgar Hoover also appears, wearing Chanel and stiletto heels. "I'm real confused," Schine whines to Cohn, who flamboyantly replies, "Of course you are, beautiful. It's the 90s!" (240). The parallels between *G. David Schine in Hell* and *Angels in America* extend beyond the presence of Cohn to include a typically Kushnerian mixing of history, fantasy, and broad humor.

The other work connected to *Angels in America* is constructed around a few characters and scenes deleted from *Perestroika* due to its length. It similarly mixes history and fantasy, as well as humor and tragedy. *Slavs! Thinking about the Longstanding Problems of Virtue and Happiness* (1994) features the old Bolshevik from the start of *Perestroika*, again demanding a theoretical basis for the future in the wake of the collapse of the Soviet Union. *Slavs!* mixes broad farce (men in drag play old babushkas, for example) and elements of fantasy with a tragic tale of a mute child dying from the effects of Chernobyl. Much of the play centers on the bittersweet relationship of a young lesbian guard at a laboratory and the doctor in charge of the facility. A coda to *Angels in America, Slavs!* presents an era of extraordinary transition that allows for a reconsideration of questions of politics, morality, race, and gender set against the sweep of history and replete with literary allusions. Aleksii Antedilluvianovich Prelapsarianov, the "World's Oldest Living Bolshevik," demands to know what "Cold Brilliant Light of Theory"[9] will replace that which has failed. A snake, he insists to the Politburo, casts off its old skin but needs a new one to replace it: "Have you, my little serpents, a new skin? Then we dare not, we cannot move ahead" (108). Debate rages while two babushkas argue over politics and Prelapsarianov collapses, a death Kushner intends—like that of Sarah Ironson at the start of *Angels in America*—to be read as symbolic, in this case representing an end to the Soviet experiment and the dawning of a moment of new possibilities. The characters wonder what new world might be created, but none can imagine it.

Shifting to those left behind to face the future without a guiding theory in the wreckage of a dead world, Kushner focuses on Katherina Serafina Gleb, a guard at the Pan-Soviet Archives for the Study of Cerebro-Cephalognomical Historico-Biological Materialism, where pickled brains of great thinkers from the Russian past reside. A directionless young woman, Katherina is pursued by a petty bureaucrat, Popolitipov, or "Poppy" as she calls him, but she cares only for Dr. Bonfila Bezhukhovna Bonch-Bruevich. Tolerating Poppy's crude advances, Katherina worries

how he may wield his power if she rebuffs him too firmly, a fear
that proves justified when Bonfila is transferred to a Siberian
medical facility for victims of the Chernobyl nuclear disaster.

Bureaucracy rears its ugly head there as Bonfila battles for
institutional support with Rodent, another oppressive func-
tionary who can provide little assistance for the unmanageable
disasters Bonfila is obliged to contend with. Her most distressing
case, Vodya Domik, an eight-year-old girl born mute as a result
of the Chernobyl nuclear disaster, will not live long. Rodent,
described as "timorous and deferential," a Soviet loyalist who
has "gotten nasty" (155), reluctantly faces Vodya's furious
mother, who demands to know what Rodent, as the government's representative, intends to do about her terminally ill
child. His dismissive response causes the furious Mrs. Domik to
recall the tragic experiences of her family as forced transplants
from Lithuania. In an expletive-laced rant, she condemns Soviet
leadership from Stalin to the present. Her enraged condemnation
of the failure of government to solve the problems created by
government silences a shaken Rodent. For contrast Kushner
focuses on Bonfila's desire, as an individual, to make a positive
difference, even in dealing with a tragedy of insurmountable and
unimaginable proportions: "In the face of all of this impossibility, twenty thousand years, that little girl who won't live five
more years, I still believe that good can be done, that there's
work to be done. Good hard work" (174). This reflection of an
activist spirit, similarly expressed in Kushner's other plays,
stresses the importance of resisting the inevitable despair that
comes after realizing that the problems at hand are too titanic
for any individual—or any government—to fix. Kushner sees
action as essential to defeat the inertia of despair and loss. Working toward the creation of a better society, however futile such

work may seem, is for Kushner the only way to survive and locate hope within hopeless circumstances. Yet the questions remain in the epilogue of *Slavs!,* which finds little Vodya, now able to speak (brilliantly), wandering in heaven where she encounters Prelapsarianov and another old Bolshevik. The old men welcome her but cannot offer wisdom when she asks, "And what sense are we to make of the wreckage? Perhaps the principles were always wrong. Perhaps it is true that social justice, economic justice, equality, community, an end to master and slave, the withering away of the state: These are desirable but not realizable on the Earth" (183). The old men and the little girl are left to ponder Lenin's question, drawn from a nineteenth-century Russian novel: "What is to be done?"

Slavs!, like *A Bright Room Called Day* and *Angels in America,* raises significant questions about the passing of old values in periods of fearful social transition, expressing a human longing for solutions to insurmountable problems, for hope where no reason for it exists, and for human connection, both through love and belonging to a community. Critics were mixed about the merits of *Slavs!,* with some expressing disappointment that Kushner's *Angels in America* follow-up seemed less ambitious. Many were approving, including Vincent Canby, who found *Slavs!* an example of a "brilliant and restless imagination. Mr. Kushner's words dazzle, sting and prompt belly laughs."[10] John Lahr noted that, even with a play smaller in structure (if not theme), Kushner "is capable of cajoling us out of our received opinions through the power of his heart and mind."[11] Few critics recognized that Kushner was experimenting with form and genre with *Slavs!,* winner of an Obie Award for best play in 1995. The play might best be described as tragic vaudeville in its combination of elements of outrageous comedy, drag, and boldly drawn caricatures with the grim realities of Chernobyl, the poignant relationship of Katherina and Bonfila, and the scalding condemnations of Mrs. Domik. These seemingly antithetical qualities intersect to express Kushner's recurrent themes more variously and uniquely than they might be expressed without such bizarre juxtapositions. As in *Hydriotaphia,* Kushner's theatricalism mixes together a wide range of serious themes and personal dilemmas, creating a strange though familiar world in which the unanswerable questions of past, present, and future coexist as both heartbreakingly real and absurdly comic.

CHAPTER 4

Homebody/Kabul

Following *Angels in America,* critics and audiences eagerly anticipated Tony Kushner's next play, expecting another epic. Aside from *Slavs!,* which was something of an addendum to *Angels in America,* and a few one-act plays, Kushner seemed to fall silent, at least in dramatic terms. Fearing what Tennessee Williams referred to as the catastrophe of success—a sharp reversal in critical approval after an unparalleled triumph—Kushner did not rush into another major production. Instead he spent time on screenplays and stage projects that did not immediately come to fruition, particularly a three-play cycle on economic history planned for production by the Royal National Theatre of Great Britain.

Kushner's particular catastrophe of success was that *Angels in America* dominated his life during the 1990s. Produced in theaters around the world and across the United States, and occasionally provoking "culture wars," *Angels in America* was a cottage industry for its author. Kushner was also occupied by several abortive starts at a cinematic version of *Angels in America,* including discussions with legendary film director Robert Altman, whose *Nashville* (1975) had, in part, inspired the multicharacter, episodic structure of *Angels in America* and, more important, its thematic sweep. With Altman, Kushner hoped to make two films encompassing the content of both *Millennium Approaches* and *Perestroika,* but no movie studio could be convinced to take up such a project. Altman moved on to other films, and the idea of an *Angels in America* film languished until HBO signed Kushner to adapt the plays as a six-hour miniseries to be directed by Mike Nichols. In the meantime Kushner worked on several projects, including a monologue, *Homebody*, for actress Kika Markham, which was produced at the fringe Chelsea Theatre Centre in London in July 1999, presumably out of the glare of the critical spotlight. Nonetheless the critics responded with nearly unanimous praise for the hour-long monologue that ultimately became the first act of *Homebody/ Kabul*, which premiered at the New York Theatre Workshop in 2001.

If *Angels in America* is a Reagan-era, state-of-the-nation play, *Homebody/Kabul* is a state-of-international-relations drama, an attempt to probe the ways America interacts with other cultures, particularly those deemed political and/or religious enemies. Kushner employed his trademark approach of interweaving titanic political and moral issues with personal lives in *Homebody/Kabul*, focusing on a dysfunctional English family caught up in the conflicts in Afghanistan, testing their notions of security and exploring the underlying issues of Western imperialism and economic dominance and exploitation of the Middle East. Examining both the rapturous and horrific moments of life in the comparatively underprivileged East seen through the eyes of these Westerners, Kushner also explores the exotic environment, the repulsion (and deep-seated fear) Westerners have for the perceived differences and savagery of the Taliban's Afghanistan, the West's exploitation of the Third World, and the rarely acknowledged guilt resulting from that exploitation. Kushner identifies toxins within the American national character (even though his characters are British), noting of the tragedies of 9/11, "We all knew this was going to happen someday. These people planned this, in this country, for years, basically out in the open. And the CIA, with a $30-billion budget, couldn't do anything?"[1] The American failure, or unwillingness, to recognize these dangers or to respond to them constructively is Kushner's starting place in a play that grieves for both American and Afghan tragedies and asks the questions that might lead to strategies of coexistence and progressive interaction among cultures in the future. *Homebody/Kabul* is a deeply political work, infused with Kushner's belief that good politics "produce good aesthetics. Really good politics will produce really good aesthetics, and really good aesthetics . . . [will] probably produce truth, which is to say, progressive politics."[2]

Homebody/Kabul also conveys a metaphysical, almost hallucinatory quality, which comes in part from the drug-induced state into which some of its characters escape. The drug use contributes to the surreal, nightmarish qualities of the Taliban's Kabul sketched from Kushner's imagination. As with *Angels in America, Homebody/Kabul* is multilayered, an intellectually complex journey, in this case into the tortured history of Afghanistan to reveal its catalytic place in twenty-first-century world politics. Kushner says he was "fascinated and concerned" for many years with developments in Afghanistan and "the sort of historical and political situation that plunges you into an examination of your own assumptions about possibility, change, the meaning of history, about your role and the country's role in the world."[3] The enormity of global social and economic injustice, and the resultant violent upheavals, may seem too complex for a single play, yet Kushner's method of framing these issues through a carefully constructed microcosm of ordinary lives allows him to illuminate the commonalities among peoples and cultures.

Inspired to some extent by Nancy Hatch Dupree's obscure 1965 guidebook, *An Historical Guide to Kabul,* published by the Afghan Tourist Organization and reprinted in 1972, which he discovered in New York University's library, Kushner begins with an awareness of Afghanistan's relation to world history, "a country so at the heart of the world the world has forgotten it."[4] Contemporary world events enhanced the significance of *Homebody/Kabul* and made Kushner appear prescient in his depiction of the country's dangers for the West, especially the United States. Acknowledging the seeming impossibility for vastly different cultures to understand each other, Kushner insists that Westerners are connected, like it or not, through a densely complex network of politics, culture, and economics to the ruptured, exploited society he depicts. Kushner's knowledge of this world, which he describes as that of a dilettante, inspires his concern with the American public's disinterest in (or ignorance of) its own foreign policy, even though 9/11 briefly awakened it. In Kushner's view the Iraq War compels Americans to consider the ramifications of decades of foreign policy decisions—that the American sense of security is illusory, stemming from a long history of economic dominance that has, in Kushner's view, led to devastating cultural collisions with no end in sight—and that may lead to more profound problems in the long term.

The tragic events of 11 September 2001 occurred just as the New York Theatre Workshop began rehearsals for the premiere of *Homebody/Kabul.* News of the play's content ignited discussion not only of Kushner's prescience but also the pertinence of questions raised in the play. Particular criticism was leveled at the appropriateness of empathizing with the "enemy" and of questioning American foreign policy as the "war on terror" began. Risking offense, Kushner announced that the play's production would go forward without changes, insisting that "even a country at war has a moral imperative to think about the people with whom they are fighting and to ask questions about them."[5] Kushner found in 9/11 the paradox of tragedy, which he believes "has a creative aspect; new meaning flows to fill the emptiness hollowed out by devastation. Are we dedicated to democratic, egalitarian principles applicable to our own people as well as to the people of the world?"[6] *Homebody/Kabul* becomes both an indictment and a progressive challenge; Kushner asks if Americans are prepared to live up to their oft-stated principles. Noting that while the Taliban carried out its atrocities during the 1990s the United States did little to stop them, only becoming concerned about the region when the losses of life and property were on American soil, one unhappy Afghan character ominously states in *Homebody/Kabul,* "You love the Taliban so much, bring them to New York! Well, don't worry, they're coming to New York!" (85).

The play illuminates the sobering and deeply disturbing realities inherent in terrorism and the subsequent Iraq War, which President George W. Bush justified by linking it to 9/11. Kushner's supposition, borne out by events, is that the prosperous West would eventually be required to weigh the meanings and lessons of 9/11, to grapple with what had precipitated this attack on the United States. The Iraq War brought those meanings and lessons into sharp focus by 2007, when Bush's popularity sank to unprecedented lows in the face of his continued prosecution of the unpopular war and of revelations that the articulated reasons for going to war were flawed if not downright wrong: Saddam Hussein, Iraq's ousted dictator, appeared to have no significant ties to the planners of 9/11, al Qaeda, and he was not secretly constructing weapons of mass destruction, as Bush claimed. Taking a resolute stance against the "axis of evil," as he described the leaders of Iraq, Iran, and North Korea, Bush adopted what Kushner described as a "cowboy mentality" in which these problems could be solved by a "shootout at the OK Corral."[7] To the suggestion that a play on this subject might seem inappropriate in the tragic aftermath of 9/11, Kushner responded, "I don't think silence is what we want to ask of artists [. . .] Although God knows there should be a certain degree of caution approaching the subject of this horror. As with Auschwitz, or the slave ships, there are places where art should only proceed with the greatest caution."[8]

Caution is not Kushner's forte, and his criticisms of the Bush administration extended to energetic participation in the unsuccessful effort to defeat Bush in the 2004 election. Kushner also crafted a scene for what may ultimately become a full-length play. *Only We Who Guard the Mystery Shall Be Unhappy* was published in the 24 March 2003 issue of the *Nation*; it depicts First Lady Laura Bush visiting a classroom to read a story to the children. An angel escorts her, and the children, all dressed in pajamas, are dead Iraqi children killed by American bombings (their pajamas are a heavenly contribution—what child, Kushner asks, does not feel safe and happy dressed in pajamas?). Mrs. Bush reads "The Grand Inquisitor" from Dostoyevsky's *Brothers Karamazov*, which, she says—as the real Mrs. Bush has said —is among her favorites. For Kushner this choice symbolizes Mrs. Bush's conflicted life. Her husband, she explains, sleeps soundly at night and she wonders how, under the tragic circumstances, he can do so. Having become a representative for beliefs markedly different from her own (she was once a Democrat and is believed to be pro-choice and against the death penalty), she despairs. Kissing the children, she quotes Dostoyevsky: "The kiss glows in my heart. But. I adhere to my ideas."[9] Culpability for Kushner also means silence in the face of a great wrong, and as such his portrait of Laura Bush indicts her silence while assailing her husband's policies.

With *Homebody/Kabul,* Kushner identifies a period of as-yet-unresolved historical transition that, as a playwright on permanent alert for such fluid moments, leads him to call for a national self-examination. Kushner considers the questions raised by the West's perception of its "enemy" and the "enemy's" perception of the West, within the complex context of present international circumstances. Rejecting notions that *Homebody/Kabul* is prescient, Kushner stresses that politically engaged artists may occasionally seem prescient when addressing contemporary political, social, and moral issues. Noting that he could "never have imagined" that the Taliban would be "gone by the time the play opened"[10]—and ultimately that the Taliban would reappear during the Iraq War (which seems to have folded Afghanistan into Iraq in Bush's mind)—Kushner eschews prescience to press concerns about the tragedies of Afghanistan under Taliban rule and about the historical and perennial conflicts in the Middle East. This focus once again places Kushner at the center of a national debate. Unfolding like a novel, *Homebody/Kabul* is a nightmarish parable illuminated by the fires burning in the Third World. As Framji Minwalla writes, Kushner's "storytelling reproduces history not as a given truth, but as a conditional way of representing the past to the present—conditional, and thus, in Brecht's sense, alterable."[11] The Brechtian connection is apt, for Kushner's play is rife with touches of theatricalism (his own brand of magic realism), allowing deconstruction of history and providing a means to inspire reconsideration of current circumstances and responses to them. Expressed through Kushner's linguistic prowess, here given a virtuosic display in the Homebody's monologue and in the various Middle Eastern dialects incorporated, characters are simultaneously life-like and iconic.

Homebody/Kabul is an over-three-hour-long examination of an intelligent, troubled, middle-class English woman's fascination with Afghanistan—and the results of that fascination. The Homebody, as she is identified, is revealed in the comfort of her cozy home, sipping tea and surrounded by her beloved books. "It is wisdom's hand which switches on the light within" (11), she explains, and the wisdom she finds most intriguing comes from travel guidebooks. An armchair traveler who has become particularly fascinated with an old Afghanistan guidebook that presents its history and circumstances without the perspective of the nation's more recent troubles, she connects with the ability to know "what *was* known before the more that has since become known overwhelms" (10). Considering the seemingly hopeless state of affairs in Afghanistan, a country destroyed by its own internal tribal strife and the incursion of capitalist and imperialist greed and war, she is poised at a safe and comfortable distance in her London living room. She formulates significant questions about the dangerous precipice upon which the Western world stands in regard to developments in Afghanistan and among its neighbors. She wonders how it is possible to interact with a culture so different from that of the West, and she questions whether it is possible to comprehend these differences from her safe environs. Is she—and, by extension, is the culture she represents—"succumbing to luxury"? (10); she wonders if Western luxury is not the most dangerous possibility of all in that it permits failure to understand the "other" and a demonizing of them, not only for truly heinous acts, but for the differences they espouse. She wonders if it is possible to feel the pain of others from comparative safety—can we only be moved by our own suffering? She even mocks herself as one who does nothing to alleviate that pain, all the while wondering if her secure world is merely an illusion. Do terrorism and the rise of the Taliban in the 1990s (and, by extension, 9/11) result from a long history of American foreign policy decisions extending back to Vietnam? Why did Western powers fail to recognize the dangers lurking within Afghanistan and the extent to which those dangers could lead to tragic outcomes? What other choices were possible, and what difference might other policies have made? Is it inevitable that these deep divisions will remain, or will the world melt into one culture, one economy, and one value system, depending upon which cultural imperatives prevail? Is such a possibility desirable? Is it possible to learn to coexist with other cultures, especially those so alien? Is religious fundamentalism impervious to compromise and peaceful coexistence? Kushner insists in *Homebody/Kabul* that there are profound consequences in the responses to these questions and that only more questions spring from each possible answer.

In *Homebody/Kabul,* as in his other major plays, Kushner ponders moments in history (and individual lives) when the prevailing circumstances unravel, when the accepted, seemingly fixed conditions become flexible. Contending that real and fundamental change may in fact be possible in such moments, Kushner posits recognition and acknowledgment of the interconnectedness among diverse, seemingly incompatible cultures, something he believes that Afghanistan, the Taliban, al Qaeda, and the resultant 9/11 attack forced the West—and the United States in particular—to confront. As he sees it, America "really can defend itself only by behaving justly with the rest of the world. If we do that, if we tackle the question of our place in the world, we can begin the new century in a spirit of transformation and justice. And if we ignore that, it'll be at our peril, and the peril of the entire planet."[12] The unstable dynamism of a chronically chaotic society or the acute turbulence of an important transition period shatters illusions of stability and, as the Homebody suggests, the danger of succumbing to luxury is similarly shattered. Society and the individual are awakened to the disturbing reality that there is no "other" in an increasingly smaller and more dangerous world. Kushner suggests that following 9/11 "something has definitely ended, and something new has begun. And I can't think of another time when this country has been called upon to examine itself, examine its responses—or rather, to examine how it should proceed in responding, which I believe should be in a circumspect and compassionate and thoughtful manner."[13] Kushner challenges America to do what may be impossible, to function in the world according to its own high ideals, noting with irony that "this country has a glorious tradition it constantly betrays"[14] and that political, religious, and economic forces are a continual danger to realizing those ideals.

That the family in *Homebody/Kabul,* which is set in 1998, is British matters little—any Westerners would do as Kushner's archetypal travelers into the East. However Kushner uses them to explore what he regards as a particularly American aversion to bad news, discomfort, difference, and instability, whether real or illusory. The Homebody insists that those living in comparable comfort and safety in the Western world are in grave danger of "succumbing to luxury" (10), and after much discussion of her own persona, her family's dysfunction (which includes emotional estrangement from her husband and her troubled daughter), her love of books (particularly travel manuals) and language, and her fantasies that, like Harper's in *Angels in America,* are partly fueled by antidepressants, the Homebody concludes that it might be better to live among the oppressed and suffering rather than to fade into a senescence of ease and security promoting inactivity in response to ideas and events, to the presumption that change can be prevented, and to the arrogance of economic power. Engagement—and a willingness to aid those without luxury—is, for Kushner, a means to avoid this fate, although in the Homebody's case, it may lead to her own demise, for she resolves to go to this faraway, dangerous land and experience it for herself.

Kushner plunges his Western Everywoman into Kabul, the epicenter of a millennial quagmire of violence and religious fundamentalism (and fanaticism), and into the welter of contradictions raised by the collision of cultures. Kushner stresses that the purposeful dramatist, who in his view is inevitably a political one, is likely to fit into one of two distinct categories: "the ones who ask small questions but give great answers (the traditionalists) and the ones who ask huge questions and often, as a consequence of the ambitiousness of their questioning, fail to give good answers or even any answers at all (the experimentalists, the vessel breakers); both are necessary."[15] There is little doubt as to which category Kushner aspires, for his political activism is firmly tied to his art and to the belief that good politics produce good aesthetics. Alert to the frayed edges of contemporary life and the pressure points of contemporary international crisis, challenging presuppositions and the clichés of political discourse, Kushner explains that no one goes to a play about Afghanistan expecting an easy night of light entertainment, adding that he depends on "an audience really wanting to ask a lot of questions and be asked to do a certain amount of thinking."[16] The interrogatory spirit is alive in his audience, he must certainly believe, for his plays demand such a spirit from them.

In *Homebody/Kabul* Kushner takes his audience into the heart of contemporary geopolitical darkness, expanding the private into the public and back again. Rife with grieving ruminations on an ancient and mysterious city now in rubble and despair, the play finds the city again at the center of a violent conflict from which it may never recover. Kushner's ruminations are a product of his politics, as well as his research and imagination, and he mixes fact with fiction to reveal the contradictions and conflicts of society through the troubled mind of his Homebody. In her monologue she recounts visiting a novelty shop, run by an Afghan man, where she purchases hats for a theme party. The hats come to represent for her a picturesque, exotic world she imagines with the aid of a guidebook; however, when she notices that part of the man's hand has been neatly chopped off, she is obliged to wonder about the reasons for this mutilation. Imagining a range of possible scenarios, including one in which she makes love to the man under an olive tree, he confides that his damaged hand results from punishment for stealing. "I stole bread for my starving family. I stole bread *from* a starving family" (23), he confesses, and Kushner implies the sliced-off hand represents imperialistic incursion into Third World culture, although the fact that the injury was inflicted by the man's own countrymen adds another layer of meaning. Kushner indicts both Third World brutality and the political and economic forces perpetuating human suffering and injustice in this image. The relativity of culpability—the notion that there is enough blame for all sides—renders the man, as Framji Minwalla writes, an "Afghan Everyman,"[17] an exemplar of the millennial international morass.

History and culture intersect in this play, as in *Angels in America,* an epic in both the classical and the Brechtian senses. Its theatrical fusing of past and present, as well as Kushner's own imaginings, demonstrate the transformative potency of theater. As James Reston Jr. writes, *Homebody/Kabul* is for "those who can see through the fog of patriotism to the finer distinctions, who are finally ready to ask how on earth do we get out of this godforsaken place, who can bear to contemplate the thought that we have participated to some extent in our own tragedy."[18] Kushner presumes his audience can bear to contemplate it, and he stresses that the idea "that nations where you have this kind of borderline anarchy and criminal behavior can be neglected is idiotic. I think what the world understands now is that taking responsibility is not an act of altruism. It's an act of self-preservation."[19]

Kushner's characters come face to face with themselves while encountering their Eastern counterparts, and all are obliged to contemplate both personal and cultural realities. Each grapples with critical choices and the consequences of these choices. The Homebody concludes her monologue as the play shifts from London to the parlous streets of Kabul. Her husband, Milton Ceiling, a repressed, middle-aged British computer specialist, and their twenty-something daughter, Priscilla, an unhappy young woman futilely seeking acceptance from her father, are attempting an uneasy truce, making a priority either finding the Homebody or claiming her remains, since Kabul officials report that she was killed walking the streets without a burka while listening to Frank Sinatra on her Walkman (in a related moment, a Kabul citizen dissolves into tears when he hears the forbidden music on the Walkman), virtually the only evidence of the Homebody's presence. Despite graphic descriptions of the mutilation of her body, there is no other indication that she is either alive or dead.

Milton, paralyzed with fear in Kabul, is inclined to accept the official explanation and sinks into an alcohol- and drug-induced daze with the assistance of Quango Twistleton, an unofficial liaison for the British government who has remained in Kabul because it provides easy access to drugs. Priscilla is not as ready to accept the official version of the Homebody's death as her father. She needs to mourn her mother, presuming the Homebody is dead, and to simply know the facts, yet she also wishes to emulate her mother. Priscilla finds empowerment in journeying forth in her mother's name. Priscilla and Milton are shocked that the Homebody appears to have courted disaster by disobeying the Taliban order and listening to her Walkman (Sinatra singing the symbolic "It's Nice to Go Trav'ling"). The Homebody has traveled all right, flown away from luxury to the harsh realities she has previously only imagined. As Milton hides in his drug-induced oblivion, Priscilla dons a burka and slips out into the frightening and exotic streets of ravaged Kabul to find her mother or answers to the mysteries surrounding her disappearance. Kushner provides no indication of what the Homebody has seen or done—and claims in interviews not to know whether she is dead or alive. Has the Homebody simply erased her previous existence or, more likely, is she exhorting Priscilla to take the leap into the forbidden and forbidding culture of Afghanistan and to learn the hard lessons to be learned from this cultural collision?

Priscilla's first lesson involves confronting the tyranny of religious fanaticism. Her encounter with Kabul under the Taliban raises questions about such extremism (not only in the Middle East, but in fundamentalism in the West), about a belief system so rigid that it leads to an embrace of—even eagerness for—martyrdom and to a disturbing ability to commit atrocities in its name. Kushner shapes this issue in service of expressing his rejection of extremist fundamentalism of any sort, incorporating veiled allusions to extreme versions of evangelical Christianity and its support of the neoconservative agenda in American politics. Fundamentalism of any sort is, in Kushner's view, inherently intolerant and, as such, a danger to progress and the pursuit of human happiness and security. He assails the Taliban for misogyny and brutality, depicting the face of religious fanaticism as implacable, unfeeling, and violent. At the same time he humanizes ordinary Afghans trapped under Taliban tyranny. Priscilla finds a local guide, a poet, who shows her the world her mother has either embraced or been destroyed by—a city, Kushner imagines in a potent metaphor, somehow cursed by the myth that the grave of the Biblical murderer Cain may reside within its borders. In an ironic twist the purported location is now a Taliban minefield, and Priscilla, wandering the figurative minefield of Kabul, learns that her mother may be alive and living as the wife of a well-to-do Muslim. This man is never seen or identified, but his Afghan wife, Mahala, is, and her rage at both the Taliban and the West is a profoundly unsettling element in the play.

Kushner's bittersweet globalism takes on an acidic edge when filtered through the persona of Mahala, a former librarian who, like the Homebody, reveres language and books. Kushner defines her by profession; to Mahala the Dewey decimal system is an international language with the goal of crossing borders to organize knowledge in coherent form. A woman of intellect and dignity, she is obliged to beg for Priscilla's help to escape Afghanistan. Her constant terror under the Taliban is causing her to forget the alphabet, an insupportable loss for an intellectual and, more particularly, a librarian. Mahala spews rage in various dialects, which Kushner uses to demonstrate the complexity of Afghanistan, where these various dialects reflect tribal diversity, a root cause of the benighted country's historic troubles. Mahala's fears do not restrain her from assailing a brutal Taliban guard: "And you call yourselves men? You suffer? We suffer more. You permit this? These criminals and savages to enslave and oppress your women? To make your women starve? You allow this? Who would allow this? You think this is Islam?" (87). Her rage may lead to her death, a fact not lost on Priscilla.

As Priscilla continues through Kabul's streets, she learns about the complex web of historical and contemporary conditions that have brought Afghanistan to its present repressive and violent state. As one character ruefully asks, "Have you noticed, nearly every other man you meet here is missing pieces?" (101). Priscilla's expanding understanding of the human tragedies deepens, and she comes to understand the rage that Mahala, a victim of the tragedies inside and outside Afghanistan, feels toward Westerners as well as her own countrymen. This fury, directed at so many things she cannot change, is reminiscent of Mrs. Domik's rage in *Slavs!* The oppressions both characters experience lead either to total resignation or an unending anger. That anger can turn inward to destroy the individual or can fuel a will to fight on. "The Present is *always* an awful place to be" (11), the Homebody says, but the struggle to make a better future provides hope—and that hope is enriched by lessons learned from the past. For Kushner the will to face the future with an activist will is a survival option, the only reasonable choice. Unlike Agnes of *A Bright Room Called Day,* Mahala (and Mrs. Domik) do not hunker down to survive the storm of catastrophe blowing over them; they rage against it, however futilely, refusing to merely accept the evil visited upon them. In Mahala's case her insistence that Priscilla and Milton get her out of Afghanistan is total; she will accept nothing short of escape. Kushner's characters are often tested by overwhelming forces, both personal and societal, and like Prior in *Angels in America,* they gain strength from their struggles if they can avoid surrendering to fear.

Some critics found it a cop-out that Priscilla and Milton (and, by extension, the audience) never find out for certain if the Homebody is dead or alive. To Kushner, though, the focus is not the Homebody, who is merely a catalyst; it is the violent collision of cultures, as the Homebody herself explains. "Ours is a time of connection; the private, and we must accept this, and it's a hard thing to accept, the private is *gone.* All must be touched. All touch corrupts. All must be corrupted" (11), she states, and it becomes evident that Kushner believes that this corrupting touch may eventually bring deeper understanding to the diverse forces that appear to be in permanent conflict. He suggests that the nearly demolished city of Kabul and the visiting Westerners are in a period of critical flux that will determine the future, for better or worse. Only Priscilla and Mahala, both of whom have been caught in the crossfire of conflicting cultures, seem to comprehend this flux as each begins the process of change made possible by the corrupting touch of their two worlds. Priscilla has lost her mother and, after a harsh confrontation, her father too, but she matures through her plunge into the surreal recesses of Kabul. She takes responsibility for saving Mahala by getting her out of Kabul along with Milton. The Homebody's favorite song, Sinatra's "It's Nice to Go Trav'ling," becomes Priscilla's mantra, and although the play ends without indicating what will become of Priscilla after her return to London, it is evident that she is transformed. Mahala ends up in London living in the Home-body's home and with the Homebody's husband, enjoying first-hand the luxuries of the West, yet she appears not to be succumbing to them. Immersion in another world and another life is the "corrupting touch" Kushner posits as a necessity for achieving a compassionate response to the "other." Making a leap into a culture or the experience of another individual is at once alien, inviting, and appalling.

Kushner finds no means to create understanding of the brutal rigidities of the Taliban, but he humanizes Afghans like Mahala and Priscilla's tour guide by empathizing with their plight. This is accomplished through what those characters reveal of their experiences and through Priscilla's yearning, desperate search for her missing mother (and perhaps for a connection to the dis-tracted Homebody that she never felt in London). Throughout Priscilla's dangerous, hypnotic search through Kabul, Kushner expands his exploration of cultural difference and emphasizes the journey to comprehension and connection the Homebody insists is essential, both among nations and between individuals. The Homebody has not been able to achieve connection with her own family, so she seeks it within an alien culture. Sinatra's "Come Fly with Me," another favorite of the Homebody, becomes a central metaphor of *Homebody/Kabul*—a musical motif representing the varied journeys of its characters. The end of the Homebody's journey is unknown, while the journeys to be made by Mahala and Priscilla remain open to speculation.

In *Homebody/Kabul,* as in his earlier works, Kushner's cen-tral concerns are most effectively delivered via his characteristi-cally voluptuous language, and the Homebody is his most obvious vehicle for this. A character for whom language is her only friend, the Homebody basks in it. "I blame it on books, how else to explain it? My parents don't speak like this; no one I know does; no one does. It's an *alien influence,* and my borders have only ever been broached by books. Sad to say" (13). This is true only until she flees to Afghanistan, where Priscilla, her comparatively inarticulate daughter, initially rejects the torrents of language her mother uses to fill an otherwise comfortably unhappy life through imaginary journeys. At the same time Priscilla is drawn to her Afghan guide, a poet, who writes what may either be poetry or intelligence for the Northern Alliance in Esperanto, a language free of the inherent cultural oppressions and burdens of history that drench other languages in blood. Esperanto is a false paradise of communication as all languages finally must be, but Kushner explores the limits of language while reveling in it, as he did with Mrs. Domik in *Slavs!* and through Louis's liberal babble in *Angels in America.* The depths of Mahala's anger cannot be fully expressed even through the range of dialects she employs to vent her rage against the Taliban and the West, both of whom, in her view, have visited misery on her country and its people.

Mahala does find the words to explain the reason for the rise of fundamentalism. Comfortably ensconced in London, she recognizes, as Priscilla puts it, that the narrow choices of fundamentalism are "what Afghanistan needs, the Taliban. Anything anything for certainty. I get the appeal of fascism now. Uncertainty kills" (138). In this Kushner, an American political dramatist, is pointing to the rise of neoconservativism during the Reagan revolution and its resurgence under George W. Bush— a troubled America is, in Kushner's estimation, seeking the resolute, black-and-white certainties emanating from the extreme version of conservatism. But such certainties may prove a dangerous comfort in fearful times, as is perhaps proved by the attitudes that led to the Iraq War, an attempt to impose one set of distinct values on a country with its own. A return to past certainties, genuine or apocryphal, is for Kushner a form of cultural denial, an avoidance of the genuine problems that will not retreat and may worsen as hollow political and moral certitudes crumble.

Ultimately *Homebody/Kabul* raises poignant, painful questions about love and connection, war, guilt, displacement, economic inequity, and the complex maze of history. Illuminating the treacherous present moment and the painful lessons the past has to teach, Kushner targets a need in his audience for "a way of addressing very deep, very intimate, very mercurial and elusive, ineffable things in a communal setting" like the theater, for art at its best "ends a certain kind of inner loneliness. Or it joins one's own loneliness with the inner loneliness of many other people. And I think that that can be healing."[20] Kushner, in the role of dramatic healer, continues his journey in *Homebody/Kabul,* a play described by critic John Heilpern as a "journey without maps to the ravaged, symbolic center of a fucked-up universe," describing the play as a towering drama about "lost civilizations and unsolvable paradoxes, furious differences and opposites and disintegrating, rotting pidgin cultures. It's about desolation and love in land-mined places, child murderers and fanatics, tranquilized existence and opium highs, travel in the largest sense of the word—travel of the mind and soul. To where? An unknowable mystery, perhaps, where all confusion is banished."[21] *Homebody/Kabul's* haunting timeliness impressed most critics and audiences during its initial run at the New York Theatre Workshop and during subsequent productions and revisions by Kushner; it reopened in revised form at the Brooklyn Academy of Music in May 2004 with Maggie Gyllenhaal as

Priscilla and Linda Emond repeating her acclaimed performance as the Homebody.

The playwright eschews the label of prophet, instead viewing his mission as twofold: (a) to incite an emotional, humanizing response to the harrowing, existential impulse toward survival in the face of the most unthinkable horrors and the most insurmountable problems, and (b) to prod vigorous discussion of strategies for navigating the political, social, and intellectual minefields of our troubled time. *Homebody/Kabul* is a dramatic response to a terrible moment in contemporary history, and it is also a plea for creating a process for humanizing the "enemy," an angry, alien "other," a process that can bring, if not a solution to unsolvable problems, at least a form of redemption for the crimes and errors of the past and some hope for a future.

CHAPTER 5

Caroline, or Change

"Nothing ever happen underground / in Louisiana / cause they ain't no underground / in Louisiana. / There is only / underwater,"[1] the title character of Tony Kushner's *Caroline, or Change* sings at the beginning of this 2003 musical drama. In the aftermath of Hurricane Katrina and the disastrous failure of the New Orleans levees to hold back the waters of the Gulf of Mexico in 2005, that city and portions of the Louisiana Gulf Coast were underwater. Responding to this seemingly eerie forecast of disaster, Kushner stresses that *Caroline, or Change* was born out of his youth in Lake Charles, Louisiana. Aside from underwater allusions, Kushner focuses attention on the economic plight of black characters who "are exactly the sort of people who couldn't get out"[2] during the post-Katrina flooding, social chaos, and death and destruction. The roots of American racism are tangled around the heart of what Kushner calls the "Hobbesian nightmare" wrought by Katrina, the failure of the government to respond to it, and what "the American Republican Party has been working hard to establish over the last 30 years: no infrastructure, no social safety net, everybody carrying a gun."[3]

Typically merging social catastrophe, politics, and lives caught up in a situation beyond individual control, Kushner writes of a specific moment in the past with parallels to contemporary travails. The soul of the American nation was tested by Katrina, a test of will and compassion typical of crisis circumstances; the nation's poor performance was exacerbated by traditional forces of economic inequity (and governmental failure), racial division, and partisan politics, all contributing to a deeper sense of alienation and hopelessness, a situation *Caroline, or Change* anticipates.

Critics registered surprise when Kushner brought forth a libretto for a musical, written in collaboration with composer Jeanine Tesori and first produced by New York's Public Theatre in 2003, particularly since the mood of this musical (which some critics described as folk opera) exuded rage, regret, disappointment, and oppression. Kushner's musical theater passions were nurtured through his family's musical roots, and as such his move in this seemingly new direction was inevitable. Kushner confesses, "I love musicals. I'm a big [Stephen] Sondheim fan. And when I was writing *Caroline,* I felt I wanted it to be set to music."[4] There is little doubt, as Kushner explains, that it is possible to "go places in a musical emotionally you can't go with just the spoken word."[5] In this musical he presents the human cost of racism to both the racist and the target of racism, proposing compassion and hope in place of despair, as he did in *Homebody/Kabul.* Kushner assesses the price of prejudice while acknowledging that racial coexistence may only be a start at truly confronting the racial divide and understanding its costs to society.

In crafting these concerns into the musical idiom, Kushner adopts a cinematic crosscutting structure similar to that which he uses in nonmusical dramas. The Brechtian influence is again central as interlocking episodes are expressed by various approaches to reveal Kushner's dominant themes. Blending American folk elements drawn from African American and Jewish American life, with aspects of Broadway kitchen-sink realism and its seeming antithesis, surreal fantasy, a new theatrical vernacular mixing music and drama is constructed. *Caroline, or Change* is a true departure from Kushner's earlier experiments with music. In the mid-1990s *St. Cecilia, or The Power of Music,* adapted from a Heinrich von Kleist story, led Kushner toward opera, but *Caroline, or Change* is undeniably a musical, albeit a pioneering one.

Kushner's major dramas and adaptations make use of blank verse, an approach not dissimilar to song lyrics, and most feature musical embellishments (for example, the mournful notes emanating from an oboe in *Angels in America* or the Homebody's affection for Frank Sinatra's singing in *Homebody/Kabul*). While New York critics found *Caroline, or Change* a musical lacking in Broadway traditions of escapist entertainment, others welcomed the attempt to merge music and serious drama to create a popular American folk style crafted from diverse musical traditions. Comparing it favorably to such diverse experimental musicals as *Porgy and Bess* and Stephen Sondheim's musical dramas, *New Yorker* critic John Lahr describes *Caroline, or Change* as a "moment in the history of theatre when stagecraft takes a new turn" in the "complexity of psychology and history" forging "a path beyond the narrative dead end of the deconstructed, overfreighted musicals of the past thirty years."[6] Kushner and Tesori eschewed Broadway spectacle, sacrificing these tools of the musical for depth of character and theme. In musical theater, where happy—or at least hopeful—endings are the coin of the realm, Kushner offers a musical of lament, a cry of the heart for what cannot be, a song of unutterable loss. A better world may be coming, but the generations that will reside in it cannot heal the sufferings of those in the past whose struggles led to that better world. Although they may mourn the suffering of those who came before, new generations cannot redeem what has been squandered, abandoned, or left to fester. Caroline Thibodeaux, the musical's central character, represents that past; a woman overlooked by society and warped by historical forces beyond her control and comprehension, Caroline is a thirty-nine-year-old black maid and single mother whose personal drama exposes the ways in which inexorable change may distort even the most ordinary life.

Caroline, or Change combines the political currents of its time with intimate personal realities, a typical device in Kushner's dramas. In this case the play is set at the watershed moment in American history of John F. Kennedy's 1963 assassination, an event Kushner believes shattered conventional perceptions of reality as well as accepted cultural values that had prevailed in the United States since World War II. Frank Rich writes that this is "a tricky mood to capture—that volatile eve of destruction before the sixties erupted into The Sixties,"[7] an era stretching into the 1970s and factoring significantly into the sociopolitical arguments of the twenty-first century. As Rich notes, the characters in *Caroline, or Change* sense that "something was going to hit them, but they didn't know what. And how could they? What was to follow in 1964 alone was unfathomable: the Beatles invasion and the overdue civil rights act, the rise of Muhammad Ali and the fall of Khrushchev, the Gulf of Tonkin resolution and the surgeon general's warning about cigarettes, the Free Speech Movement in Berkeley and the KKK's murders of Chaney, Goodman and Schwerner in Mississippi."[8] In fact Kennedy's murder initiated a decade of unprecedented turmoil and change that included America's military involvement in Vietnam and its cataclysmic withdrawal, the political assassinations of Malcolm X, Martin Luther King Jr., and Robert F. Kennedy, the Watergate scandal, and the aftermath of all of these cultural tremors. In Kushner's lyrics a couple of anthropomorphic characters wonder, "What lies in store in Nineteen-Sixty-Three? Or Four?" (13); his millennial audience knows only too well.

Caroline, or Change depends, to some extent, on images of the socially conscious "race films" of the 1950s and 1960s, films such as *Black Like Me, Imitation of Life, Lilies of the Field, Guess Who's Coming to Dinner?* and *In the Heat of the Night.* In this and other aspects, *Caroline, or Change* reflects major changes in popular culture, although most of these films focus on extraordinary, even heroic black characters, whereas Caroline is not an extraordinary woman (although it is clear that she could be much more if given a chance) and her circumstances are commonplace. Kushner confronts the well-worn terrain of the sixties in a unique way. First he begins with what he considers its inciting event (JFK's murder), and then, more significantly, he focuses on Caroline, a maid for a middle-class family of New York Jews recently transplanted to Louisiana. The shifting tectonic plates of American life are envisioned through Caroline's experience at a moment when her life, and the lives of those around her, reflects and frames as-yet-unarticulated issues arising from the social transitions just beginning. Bitter and emotionally distant, Caroline clings to religious faith and the rules of the Jim Crow world she knows, finding herself in a complex relationship with Noah Gellman, the eight-year-old son of her employers. A lonely, confused boy struggling to deal with the death of his mother and attempts by a well-meaning stepmother to fill the void, Noah turns to Caroline, "Caroline our maid! / Caroline! Caroline! Caroline / the President of the United States!" (14). He sees her as an all-knowing, powerful figure, "who's stronger than my dad" (14), a stable force during the time his little world has radically changed.

The small events in the lives of Caroline, Noah, and their families ultimately loom large as Kushner honors the importance of the ordinariness of their experiences. Caroline is a single mother struggling to raise her children on too little money, no opportunity, and with only faith to cling to—although religion proves an increasingly unsatisfactory refuge as her sense of hopelessness and dissatisfaction mounts. Noah is grappling with his loss and flailing around for guidance; his father, Stuart, is emotionally remote and withdrawn in the aftermath of his wife's death. Despite the fact that Stuart has recently married Rose Stopnick, his late wife's friend, he has not reentered life and, as such, cannot help his unhappy son. Immersed in music, Stuart expresses his feelings through his clarinet, exuding musical grief much like the mournful oboe underscoring *Angels in America*. When Noah wonders why God would take his mother, Caroline explains that God made her cancer and that it is God's way of eating people when he chooses. Stuart's numbed response to Noah's questioning of this grim metaphor is only "your mother is dead / and there is no God" (22). Noah resists Rose, who is seeking a precarious place within this little broken family. To assert herself and provide structure for Noah, she zeroes in on his failure to empty change from pockets before throwing his clothes in the laundry. The two collide in a seriocomic battle of wills, but loose change looms larger for the prideful Caroline when Rose decides that Noah's punishment will be that Caroline may keep money she finds in Noah's pockets. The seeming innocuousness of this represents for Kushner the blood-red meat of racial division in America; Noah's change means little to him, while for Caroline it makes a real difference. Her dilemma about taking the money becomes a central metaphor for the imbalance of economic and political power between white and black America.

Kushner's depiction of 1960s Louisiana has a basis in historical reality as well as in autobiography, but these realities are couched in a dramatic underworld in which anthropomorphic characters—a washing machine and dryer, the moon, a radio, and a city bus—sing the blues for Caroline's struggle, Noah's grief, and the national agony at the moment of Kennedy's death. It is a world in which an errant twenty-dollar bill reveals changes within the social dynamic at a moment of cultural transition. As with *A Bright Room Called Day, Hydriotaphia, Angels in America, Slavs!,* and *Homebody/Kabul,* Kushner juxtaposes real and imaginary elements to frame issues without easy answers. Kushner also grieves for that which cannot be changed and for those trapped in an unhappy past; as in prior works, he imagines a world where the fine distinctions of racial and ethnic diversity, religious belief, and morality may not necessarily divide American society, while acknowledging the sad past that may be partially redeemed through its ability to provide lessons for negotiating the present and constructing a future. Turning a corner toward a point of no return is as frightening as it is inevitable, and the search for clarity and closure springs from fear as much as from a desire for a neat and complete solution. Closure also implies an unchangeable ending, a situation that is permanent. Kushner is not convinced that closure, in either a societal event or an individual's life, exists or is even a desirable goal. Change, in his view, is inevitable and progressive; *Caroline, or Change* dramatizes the terrifying and, at the same time, exhilarating moment when tumultuous change allows a reconsideration of a life and of the social contract.

The idea of change invites Caroline and Noah out of the nightmare darkness into a new life, a plunge like that made by Nora Helmer of Henrik Ibsen's *A Doll's House.* On the postmodern stage, courageous plunges are as emotionally complicated as Caroline and Noah's situations suggest, but sociopolitical implications are less black-and-white. Nora can be said to be seeking equality in a society egregiously inequitable as to women's rights, but the social inequities Caroline faces suggest possible correctives far more complex. Kushner asks if a society or a life must be shattered so that it may be rebuilt. Embracing change is enticing and frightening, as exemplified by Nora on the other side of the famous door she slammed at the end of *A Doll's House;* for Caroline the shattering of her life may leave her with nothing but her losses, a dilemma posited in her concluding aria, "Lot's Wife."

Kushner expresses these concerns through a deceptively simple plot and through the play's central character. Divorced, uneducated, and the mother of four children (the eldest of whom is on the firing line in Vietnam), Caroline regards change as her nemesis. She clings to an ethos of hard work and Christian moral righteousness, conscientiously doing her job, remaining uncompromisingly herself and refusing to play the smiling, complacent family retainer of southern "Mammy" stereotypes. The prevailing social contract forces her to work at a menial job for scandalously small pay (Rose acknowledges this at one point), and Caroline laments this fact in song: "Been twenty-two years of cleaning. / For all them years I worked and prayed. / Every day I doing laundry, / thirty-nine and still a maid" (17). Only earning thirty dollars a week, she has barely enough to survive on, with nothing left for hope.

Caroline is certainly no "Mammy" in the cinematic tradition of Hattie McDaniel. Kushner takes pains to push Caroline, whose persona was inspired by Kushner family maid Maudi Lee Davis, in the opposite direction of the stereotype of a black woman in a crisp, white maid's uniform. As Tonya Pinkins, who played Caroline in its original Public Theater, Broadway, and London productions, explains, the "arc of the character is Greek in proportion,"[9] and "I think she's a woman who is bigger than the life she is given to live."[10] Caroline is street smart, sharp tongued, and angry with the God she fervently believes in, who seems to have forgotten her. A vigorous work ethic and moral rigidity cannot fend off the despair slowly destroying Caroline's spirit. Kushner expresses frustration that some critics "thought we were going for a big sort of Mammy story but we blew it and they didn't get that *Caroline* is an attempt to turn that on its head,"[11] to reconstruct this iconic figure as a fully dimensioned human being discontented with the role society demands she play. The Mammy trope aside, Kushner stresses that "Caroline is a woman who loses her mobility. She can't stop grieving over losses, and, like [Walter] Benjamin's angel, her face is turned to the past. She wants to go back, but the terrible lesson of history is that she can't."[12] She cannot move forward either; things are changing, the stasis she has been mired in (and clings to) is shifting, but she cannot see a place for herself in the new order. To survive her grief, Caroline closes off her emotions; she goes on but in a detached state in which she can function in the muteness of domestic slavery, a slavery not ended for black women even a hundred years after the Civil War. As Prior realized in *Angels in America,* there are individuals who live past hope, and Caroline's steely resolve is required for her to live past the death of hope. Unable to imagine a better future, Caroline bitterly clings to faith and gives up illusions, including even harmless fantasies of nocturnal visits from Nat King Cole. In the steamy Gellman basement, her own personal purgatory, she floats in suspended animation below the water table.

The dichotomy, and tension, of Caroline's character lies in the juxtaposition of her great pride with her role as a servant. In the combustible times of Kennedy's assassination, Caroline is submerged, a member of one of the lost generations of African Americans who lived before social changes remade racial boundaries in the 1960s. Caroline can only imagine a future she cannot be part of: "Some folks do all kind of things and / black folks someday live like kings / and someday sunshine shine all day! / Oh sure it true / it be that way / but not for me" (117), she sings in "Lot's Wife." The character of Caroline is a true tour de force, with wells of suppressed rage and desperation at once compelling and unsettling. "Lot's Wife" is not a traditional "eleven o'clock number" in the Broadway musical tradition, but a grim, raging account of the sacrifices of a stagnant life by one at the bottom of the social order. Kushner's scalding lyrics, supported by Tesori's music, lift Caroline to heroic heights, transforming her into an icon of survival and self-awareness. Despite Caroline's inability to change, she recognizes the depth of her own inner turmoil. Her despair—and the ultimate tragedy of those she represents—finds full voice as she cries out for an end to the life she must live: "Murder me God down in that basement / Murder my dreams so I stop wantin', / murder my hope of him returnin', / strangle the pride that make me crazy / Make me forget so I stop grievin. / Scour my skin till I stop feelin. / Take Caroline away cause I can't be her, / take her away I can't afford her. / Tear out my heart / strangle my soul" (118).

Caroline's pain causes her to resist the very changes she desires and that are so palpably in the air, but her daughter Emmie, a budding activist, can envision a different future, as can Caroline's friend Dotty, another maid who attends college at night to build a better life. Caroline wants a better life too, but it is too late—she longs for change she no longer believes is possible for her. Change metaphors leapfrog over each other as changes of every sort—social, political, economic, personal, spiritual—take place in the lives of the main characters. Early on, the moon sings, "Change come fast and change come slow / but change come, Caroline Thibodeaux" (32), but Caroline can't afford change: the constraints of oppression have taught too many hard lessons. And Noah too, who reaches out to Caroline, suffers from changes he cannot control, especially his mother's death and the appearance of a stepmother, a decent woman he cannot find a way to love. The ways in which an individual negotiates life as historical changes carry her or him into the future emphasize Kushner's conception of change. The world, like personal lives, cannot be permanently fixed; its status is always negotiable, and change is accompanied by struggle, pain, and fear of the unknown. In this respect the play's title has many meanings, referring most literally to the coins Noah leaves in his clothes. Rose's invitation to Caroline to keep the change, a seemingly simple cure for Noah's carelessness, leads to a shattering exposure of cultural conflicts. Change is not just coins; it is social change in America of the early 1960s, as well as personal changes faced by Noah, who has lost his mother and is adrift, and Caroline, whose bitterness and despair make it impossible for her to embrace the changes that will improve life for her children, if not for her. The only changes Caroline has known—the desertion of her husband and the possible death of her eldest son in Vietnam—have diminished her, and the positive changes Dotty and Emmie represent are out of reach for a woman who works for the equivalent of pocket change.

Noah reaches out to Caroline, but despite surface similarities, *Caroline, or Change* is not *The Member of the Wedding,* in which a family's black maid provides warmth and comfort. Noah's aching for a surrogate mother and a sense of himself in the world may call to mind the comforting stereotypes of such southern coming-of-age literature, but Caroline places limits on how much she will nurture Noah. She allows him to light her cigarettes and hang out with her in the basement laundry room, where she occasionally offers a form of tough love, as Noah's assessment of their relationship explains: "My mama liked you! / I do too! / You're implacable, / indestructible, Mama said. / I'm always sad. / I like it that you're always mad" (46). Kushner, who based Noah on aspects of himself and his brother Eric, calls *Caroline, or Change* a "mis-memory"[13] play in which Noah's neediness is only the beginning of a more complex psychological struggle for Noah and Caroline and within each of their troubled souls.

Kushner says that *Caroline, or Change* is "the closest to autobiography of anything I've done,"[14] although it is autobiographical only in essences, with the shards of real people he reassembles as characters incorporating imagined elements as well. Kushner's own mother, for example, did not die until he was a grown man—the chronology is different, but the emotional pain of her loss radiates through the musical. One can certainly imagine Kushner as Noah, an intellectually precocious child, growing in political awareness, skeptical about religion, and confused about sexuality (for example Noah confesses that he secretly plays with Barbie dolls, the only indication of his latent homosexuality). Like most children Noah is a mystery to himself, although his uncommon intelligence and the burdens of loss he carries are not typical. Noah is captured in a moment of great bewilderment—he has lost his mother, and over the course of the story, he loses Caroline, the surrogate mother he longs for but cannot reach. His feelings may also have a preadolescent, semitropical quality, as he reaches out to Caroline during moonlit nights, imagining being with her and her family, although he may only wish to be her child. At the very least Noah and Caroline are joined by shared grief that neither can articulate. In Noah's world there is a comfortable *Leave It to Beaver* set of values and daily routine, but beneath this thin veneer are deep emotional wounds that, along with those felt by his father and by the stepmother who struggles to connect with him, imbue the surface ordinariness of their lives with an aching sense of loss.

Kushner transforms Caroline's financial need and Noah's emotional neediness into the personal economics of *Caroline, or Change,* where Rose's lesson about Noah's careless disregard for his money has a profound impact on them both. In Noah's mind he transforms the situation into a pass into Caroline's life, imagining what she and her children do with his money. He thus becomes a member of their family, even calling himself Noah Thibodeaux. Caroline keeps her distance, acknowledging the separate but unequal worlds coexisting in the Deep South in that period. Even so she sadly notes the profound emotional connections between them: "That sorrow deep inside you, / it's inside me, too, / and it never go away" (124).

The relationship between Caroline and Noah allows Kushner to tap into the long love-hate history of blacks and Jews in America, a cultural intersection that occasionally flares into violence. Although a few black-Jewish "buddy" plays, like *The Zulu and the Zayda, I'm Not Rappaport,* and *Driving Miss Daisy*, have appeared with attention focused on the oppressions both groups have experienced, this fractious relationship has rarely been explored in mainstream American drama. In *Caroline, or Change,* the Gellmans understand oppression from their own experiences as liberal New York Jews plunked down in the midst of an unwelcoming community, weaving another thread into the complex issues of loss, class difference, and racial and ethnic division probed through the small struggles of the mournful, symbiotic odd couple of Caroline and Noah. The tenuous bond of these two displaced souls breaks apart at the muted holidays following Kennedy's assassination. Stopnick, Rose's father and a 1930s-style socialist, gives Noah a crisp twenty-dollar bill as his Hanukkah gelt, insisting that the boy contemplate the meaning of the money and what work it could do in the world. Stopnick could hardly imagine the impact of his socialist economics on Noah. It also forces a severe test on Caroline when Noah leaves the cash in his pocket. His forgotten change has allowed her to buy treats for her children, but twenty dollars could make a genuine difference, and she keeps it. Noah confronts Caroline, demanding his money, and when she stands her ground, both lose their tempers, leading him to recklessly play the race card. He wildly suggests that President Lyndon B. Johnson has created a bomb to kill all Negroes; to this Caroline responds in kind but returns Noah's twenty dollars, lamenting that the "money reach in and spin me about, / my hate rise up, rip my insides out" and, worst of all as she sees it, "Spoke my hate to a child. / Pennies done that" (116).

This climactic scene between Noah and Caroline calls to mind Athol Fugard's *Master Harold . . . and the Boys,* a drama in which another young white boy asserts social dominance over nurturing black elders, regretting it even as he does so. An immature child, Noah may not fully understand what he has done, and he longs to make amends with Caroline. "Weren't never friends" (123), she honestly replies, but as is typical of Kushner's drama, the future remains an open question. For the short term this sad encounter plunges both Noah and Caroline into solitary sadness. In her case the bleakness of her reality and hopelessness of her future weigh more heavily than before. She cannot bring herself to return to the Gellmans' house for days, seeking solace at church, even as she knows she must ultimately return to a job she does not want. Her economic need is too great, her children must be fed, the rent must be paid, and as she always has, Caroline must surrender to reality.

For Noah's part, having driven away the one comforting constant in his life, he faces an even lonelier future, although his pain finally allows him to let Rose offer comfort. In the moonlight Caroline speaks to Noah's pain, allowing that "Someday we'll talk again / but they's things we'll never say" (124). It is possible they can forge a new relationship, but both can only do it through change. Change may be possible for young Noah and for Caroline's children, but it will not be possible for Caroline. All the characters in *Caroline, or Change* are facing changes; some, like Caroline herself, cannot (or will not) change, while others move forward. Dotty pursues education as a means of creating options for herself, embracing cultural changes from new music to trendy clothes, while the immovable Caroline disapproves, bluntly telling Dotty, "I don't like the way you do. / You change" (29). The benighted Rose tries hard to win a place in Noah's heart—and to draw her still-grieving husband out of his isolation. Her consistently rebuffed attempts to love Noah and befriend Caroline keep her in an angst-ridden state, struggling vainly to make a new family of the Gellmans. She finally wins a small victory when Noah turns to her after his devastating encounter with Caroline. For Noah the first step into mature adulthood can be taken now that the frozen emotions following his mother's death are beginning to melt. Losses, however devastating, must be grieved for and accepted; life must go on, and changes may open new doors. Kushner insists that the journey forward comes with the understanding that losses are inevitable and that life is a continual process entailing loss. Caroline's stasis, like that of Agnes in *A Bright Room Called Day*, means she only has grief (and rage) to sustain her if she cannot change.

The losses of the personal lives of the characters reflect national losses. Kushner states that the changes in mid-1960s America were felt more slowly in the South he knew while growing up in Lake Charles, Louisiana, where "change was taking place, of course, but in a more subterranean fashion, and at a different pace, than elsewhere in America."[15] Regardless of the pace, social changes hang heavily over *Caroline, or Change,* as spectral presences hang over the lives of its characters. Noah's late mother, Caroline's absent husband, and the son Caroline may never see again, not to mention the historical figures of Kennedy, King, and Johnson, among other iconic personages of the sixties, create a potent atmosphere. Kennedy's assassination is the incident that sets the play into motion and is felt deeply by the characters. "Our almost friend is gone away," some lament, "The earth, the earth has bled, / The president / Oh blight November winter night / the president is dead" (34). For Caroline, Kennedy's death is a personal devastation, since he epitomizes hope. His tragically short time in the White House meant that the liberal optimism he exuded was never realized. He is a historical floater, always there as a reminder of what might have been if he had lived to fulfill his hopeful rhetoric. Caroline must face up to a future with the loss of the hope Kennedy personified. His death also suggests that the country is an "Orphan Ship of State! / Drifting! Driverless!" (34).

The only character seemingly unmoved by Kennedy's death is Emmie, Caroline's spitfire daughter, who sings, "I ain't got no tears to shed / for no dead white guy" (43). Emmie is more than prepared to embrace the changes in the air and to soldier forth to forge a better world. She will not look to white America; she looks to herself and to the black community for strength. Finding true liberation in this choice, Emmie gains strength, although she comes to realize that her mother may not be able to navigate the confusions of social change. Emmie, with her younger brothers in tow, charges into the new world not only for herself, but to redeem her mother's backbreaking, heart-wrenching life. Emmie has all the freed force Caroline cannot release from herself except in solitary rage and grief; Emmie thus becomes Caroline's fulfillment even though Caroline does not grasp it. In fact she warns Emmie away from hope: "Don't give yourself options. / Most folks live without em" (41). Para-doxically Caroline is Emmie's model for change, for Caroline and her generation are necessary for Emmie's generation to fully grasp their own circumstances and what the social changes por-tend. The suffering that has come before is transformed into fuel for change. In a sense *Caroline, or Change* is a tribute to Caroline's generation, those who could see and feel the coming changes, yet were locked out, firmly tied to the Jim Crow past. As Emmie bluntly puts it: "They's people who freeze / while they wait on their knees / and they don't know for what / and they just been forgot / and I / ain't waitin no more" (96). Emmie provides the fiery heart and activist spirit of *Caroline, or Change;* her eye is on the future, on a world of newfound pos-sibilities for a young black woman in a society still far from pro-viding equality for African Americans, but closer to it than even she dreams possible.

Throughout *Caroline, or Change* Kushner constructs parallel circumstances, points up contrasts, sets his characters into episodic encounters in which he shifts allegiances; it is a work in which every situation or emotion is countered by its opposite. Exploring the contradictory nature of existence and the collapse of absolutes, Kushner exposes the dangers of cultural conformity through small subdramas among various subsets of characters, such as a heated debate between Stopnick and Emmie over the merits of Martin Luther King's policy of nonviolence policy. It is not a predictable story of uplift typical of pop-culture encounters with issues of self-esteem, class struggle, and tacit racism. Instead, through an unsparing examination of the emotional core of each character and the society in which it is set, *Caroline, or Change* reinvigorates the race debate in drama. Linking its characters through realistic and theatrical elements, the play releases the fierce humanism locked inside the suspended emotions and fears of its characters to set in motion spiritual regeneration.

As such the choice of the musical form is logical; music is a means of expressing emotion for characters otherwise unable to articulate their feelings, and it is a manifestation of the human spirit. Kushner originally intended to write *Caroline, or Change* as an opera, and in the final analysis, it may be one, at least in the sense that there is little dialogue. Perhaps best described as a "sung-through" musical, the lyrics are supported by Tesori's musical themes, which are inspired by a range of musical idioms, including Mozart, Motown, klezmer, gospel, rhythm and blues, Kurt Weill, Aaron Copland, and Broadway. It aims for a wholly original sound abstracted from the various forms of language and music of the 1960s and before. Kushner's lyrics evoke a southern lyricism, from the musicality of street speech to its literary heritage, and the dialects of his Jewish background are central in depicting the Gellmans and Stopnick. Some critics found it difficult to catch all of the subtleties in one hearing, but many acknowledged the novel exploitation of musical form stretching from the dawn of American musical theater through Brecht and Weill and on to Sondheim. Advertised in its premiere at New York's Public Theater as "a new musical on the search for hope, identity and the American soul," Kushner himself described it as "a piece in some ways about death and loss, but it's quite exuberant and extremely melodic. It certainly isn't grim or atonal."[16]

Critical praise was directed at the anthropomorphic characters of *Caroline, or Change*. Caroline's companions in the hot, airless confines of the basement laundry room include a radio—voiced by a trio modeled on the Supremes—a washer, and a dryer, which taunts her to "turn it on, turn on despair!" (16). Caroline's despair is reflected by these singing appliances, as well as by a city bus that laments Kennedy's assassination and by the moon, a musical catalyst for Caroline's nocturnal fantasies and conversations with Noah. Both Noah and Caroline are able to expose their true feelings and emotional disorder and longings with the moon's encouragement. These oddly whimsical anthropomorphic creatures, perhaps imagined as a result of Kushner's affection for children's literature (among his earliest works are children's plays) and the fact that one of his central characters is a child, led to a collaboration with children's author and illustrator Maurice Sendak on the opera *Brundibár* first at the Chicago Opera Theater, followed by New York performances in 2006 at the New Victory Theater. *Brundibár,* with music by Czech composer Hans Krása, was premiered at a Jewish boys' orphanage in 1942, after which Krása and the conductor Rudolph Freudenfeld were sent to the Theresienstadt concentration camp, which the Nazis promoted as a model Jewish ghetto. *Brundibár* was performed fifty-five times at the camp, providing comfort to its inmates as well as Nazi propaganda. Kushner's libretto, adapted from the original by Adolf Hoffmeister, is a somber account of two children trying to get milk for their sick mother. The children sing for pennies, but are drowned out by the organ grinder Brundibár ("bumble bee" in Czech), a symbolic Hitler figure, who wants the money. With the help of several animals, the children create a chorus to drown out Brundibár. Well received by critics, *Brundibár* reflects similar questions of economics and power explored in *Caroline, or Change*.

Critics such as John Lahr pointed to dramatic innovations in *Caroline, or Change* that take "the musical back to storytelling, to a moral universe, to a dissection of American society, both black and white, which Zora Neale Hurston called 'the boiled-down juice of human living.'"[17] Kushner's nonmusical works are typically liberated from realism through phantasmagoric elements, ghostly characters, and by treating the stage as a realm between the real and the imaginary where anything is possible. In musical form Kushner carries this liberation further, allowing characters access to each other's worlds, thoughts, and feelings, as in the moonlit encounters of Caroline and Noah. This happens most overtly when Noah imagines himself a singing and dancing member of Caroline's family, doo-wopping the song "Roosevelt Petrucius Coleslaw." In the way Prior and Harper met in a mutual hallucination in *Angels in America,* Noah is able to will himself into Caroline's world. This crossover is also a reminder of the sort of cross-cultural appropriation typical of the musical stage in America from its birth, where Jewish entertainers like Al Jolson or Eddie Cantor put on blackface to sing "coon songs"—a way of abandoning one oppressed persona to take on another and of celebrating all oppressed minorities, even if the cultural appropriation is undeniably racist. Part racism, part homage, part cultural theft, part integration of racial and ethnic diversity in "a melting pot where nothing ever melted,"[18] as Kushner's Rabbi Chemelwitz describes it in *Angels in America,* blackface came to represent racist attitudes. Despite melting-pot analogies, races and ethnicities do not conveniently collapse into one another as such cultural appropriation might imply. Blissfully unaware of all this, Noah merely longs to be in Caroline's family, and Kushner allows music to carry him there.

Music aside, Kushner derives potent linguistic effects from the use of simple, ordinary words—change, underground—much as he enlivens mundane household items—a washer, a dryer, a radio —to lend significance to that which is seldom considered as having any. *Caroline, or Change* also focuses on the domestic world of women and children, those in traditional mid-twentieth-century America considered to belong to a comparatively insignificant realm. For Kushner this represents another form of disenfranchisement, a lack of access to a fully realized expression of self. Brewing social changes may become evident slowly and in unexpected ways, Kushner posits, and these may be sensed in ordinary family life. In the way that Susan Glaspell's *Trifles* reveals through overlooked domestic details the reasons an abused woman murders her husband, *Caroline, or Change* conjures telling images of cultural issues through a seemingly minor domestic conflict between a despairing black maid and a lonely little boy.

Reviewers grappled with the magical enlivening of the everyday into the profound through the anthropomorphic characters, which some considered a distraction. John Simon, a conservative critic who had condemned Kushner's prior works including *Angels in America,* claimed that Kushner "bites off more than he can chew"[19] in *Caroline, or Change,* yet such a dismissal misunderstands Kushner's style. He typically bites off more than he can chew to raise a range of questions on human experience, political exigencies, and the longing for transcendence central to postmodern American life. Michael Feingold found that *Caroline, or Change* was "the first post-Structuralist musical"[20] while insisting that Kushner's Brechtian tendencies fend off emotional access to the characters. Like those critics who dismissed Sondheim's musical dramas on similar grounds in the 1960s and 1970s, Feingold misses the point, mistaking intellectual rigor for emotional alienation. Emotional payoffs are earned through a complexity and depth not typical of usual musical theater positivism; Kushner steadfastly avoids surface (and unearned) displays of uplift that enliven most musicals. To some critics *Caroline, or Change* seemed too brooding and serious to compete with lighthearted musical fare like *Hairspray* and *Avenue Q,* both of which were on Broadway at the same time. Despite critical disagreement, which included a guardedly respectful review from Ben Brantley, the all-important *New York Times* critic, audiences were drawn to *Caroline, or Change.* When it opened at the Public Theater, it dominated the off-Broadway scene during late 2003. The question of the survivability of such an atypical musical on Broadway caused hesitation for its producers, who finally announced in early 2004 that *Caroline, or Change* would move to Broadway's Eugene O'Neill Theater, where it reopened on 2 May 2004 (following previews). It managed a four-month run and was recorded by Hollywood Records on a two-CD set, preserving the entire show. The musical has since been produced by regional theaters, and its 2006 London production, with Tonya Pinkins recreating her performance as Caroline, won the 2007 Olivier Award as best musical.

Like *Angels in America, Caroline, or Change* digs deeply into the open wounds of post–World War II America, searching the vistas of modern history and the social canvas for neglected corners of experience as a way of understanding the changing rhythms of the American landscape. In looking to the ordinary and personal, Kushner illuminates the anxiety of change, along with the psychological and historical realities of change, with visceral force. Emphasizing the painful personal transitions implicit in conflicted times, Kushner memorializes the dead, forgotten, and disenfranchised while sifting through the historical ruins for remnants of hope; as with all his plays, lessons are to be learned from what has passed and what has been suffered. He looks for unforeseen consequences emerging from national tragedy and the ordinary lives it affects, in the process locating unspoken emotional concerns and political tensions clinging to them. In doing so he recognizes what Dotty tells Caroline, that it hurts to change, "it feel like you got to break yourself apart, / it feel like you got to break your own heart, / but / folk do it. They do" (115).

CHAPTER 6

Adaptations

Tony Kushner won critical attention with *Angels in America* and subsequent similarly epic dramas, but his first major works for the stage were adaptations of classics. His first widely produced adaptation, Pierre Corneille's seventeenth-century comedy *L'illusion comique*, retitled *The Illusion* when Kushner's free adaptation was first performed in 1988, is a pared-down, two-act rehab of a rarely revived play. Kushner added several scenes of his own to extend thematic chords only hinted at in Corneille's original. The resulting hybrid at once celebrates and lampoons neoclassical comedy, mocking its flowery speeches, play-within-a-play conceit, and formulaic romantic plotting while also exploiting these techniques.

The Illusion functions on multiple levels, most obviously as a two-act meditation on theater and the value of illusion and storytelling. "The art of illusion," one of Kushner's characters quips, "is the art of love, and the art of love is the blood-red heart of the world,"[1] a poignant notion allowing an examination of the vagaries of love through a miserable old man's search for the son he banished years before. Kushner does not simply adapt Corneille's play, he reconstructs it, as he did with other neglected works by great writers. Only in the case of Bertolt Brecht, whose dramas, theories, and politics profoundly influenced Kushner's aesthetic, has he tended to be faithful to the original. The theatrical past permits Kushner a rich resource of themes, emotions, and images of human experience, not to mention techniques, to draw from in his progress toward a more presentational style than the traditions of modern realistic drama might seem to permit.

The Illusion's unsympathetic protagonist, Pridamant, is a cantankerous old fool who turns to a magician, Alcandre, as he feels his life ebbing away. Longing for his estranged son, despite insisting otherwise, he watches in amazement, joy, and horror as the magician conjures up scenes depicting the son in three circumstances, curiously identified by different names in each. These episodes focus on sundry romantic misadventures in differing moods, with the changes in name and other disjunctures disorienting Pridamant. In a Kushner addition to Corneille, Alcandre explains, "My visions are concocted through a violent synthesis, a forced conflation of light and shadow, matter and gossamer, blood and air. The magic's born of this uneasy marriage; it costs, you see, it hurts, it's dragged unwillingly from the darkest pools" (50). Alcandre tauntingly invites Pridamant to give in to "the strange, pulsing warmth; the flow of blood, the flood of time, immediate, urgent, like bathing water in a warm ocean, rocked by currents of disappointment, joy. . . . The heart chases memory through the cavern of dreams" (50), while the old man shifts from anger at his son's less-than-admirable behavior to empathy when the boy's struggles seem unfairly overwhelming. Pridamant's regrets and love for his errant son unsettle him, and he shows signs of vulnerability when a lone crystalline tear drops from his eye. Achieving his end of touching Pridamant's cold heart, Alcandre reveals that the images of the son are merely scenes from plays; the son, it turns out, is an actor. "I don't know that I like that," Pridamant grumbles, complaining that the theater is "a make-believe world" consisting "of angel hair and fancy talk, no more substantial than a soap bubble. You are moved at the sight of a foul murder—then the murderer and the murdered are holding hands, taking bows together. It's sinister" (81). Alcandre passionately disagrees in another Kushner amendment: "What in this world is not evanescent? What in this world is real and not seeming?" (81); these theatrical illusions show, Alcandre insists, that "love is a sea of desire stretched between shores—only the shores are real, but how much more compelling is the sea. Love is the world's infinite mutability; lies, hatred, murder even are knit up in it; it is the inevitable blossoming of its opposites, a magnificent rose smelling faintly of blood. A dream which makes the world seem . . . an illusion" (82). Confused, Pridamant wanders away as Alcandre literally exposes the rickety trappings of an old stage.

New York Times reviewer David Richards writes appreciatively that the play's "cosmic touch springs from Mr. Kushner's fecund imagination, not Corneille's,"[2] an apt point since the philosophical reflections on love's travails are almost exclusively Kushner's, as are numerous jibes at theatrical artifice and father-son relationships. He respects Corneille's structure while avoiding pitfalls of reverence or overemphasis on contemporary theatrical requirements. *The Illusion,* in Kushner's hands, becomes a bittersweet illusory romance on love in myriad moods, in essence tying it to a central thematic chord running through Kushner's original works, as can be seen in the shattering pain experienced by Prior and Harper when abandoned by the men they love in *Angels in America,* in Priscilla's anguish over parental disapproval in *Homebody/Kabul,* and in Noah's aching loss following his mother's death in *Caroline, or Change.* Love is hard in Kushner's world; its joys are tempered by pain. Without pain, he asks, how joyful can the joy be?

Kushner's adaptations of two works from the German classical period further illustrate themes raised in *The Illusion*. For example, adapting Johann Wolfgang von Goethe's little-known 1776 romantic drama *Stella* (revised by Goethe in 1806), Kushner extends *The Illusion*'s intimate exploration of the difficult path of lovers and the varied forms love can take. A lifelong student of German literature, Kushner found in this romance a vehicle for themes of continuing importance to his own plays. Kushner's adaptation, *Stella: A Play for Lovers,* was first performed at the New York Theatre Workshop in 1987, and he continues to revise it. *Stella* has enough intricate plotting and emoting for a grand opera. The structure, characters, and themes of Goethe's play are not altered significantly by Kushner, who instead sharpens the delicate text with the aim of drawing out universal relevance. A forerunner of the morally ambiguous, sexually charged plays of Arthur Schnitzler, *Stella* depicts the pains and joys of love (and the complications of sex) by blending lyrical and cynical language in both tragic and comic interludes. Injecting a postmodern viewpoint, Kushner trims and reshapes the play's dialogue into an expression of tragicomic romance. Goethe's plot, maintained in its entirety, centers on Cecilia, a woman abandoned by her husband, who arrives in a small town with her daughter, Lucy. The daughter is to become companion to Stella, a baroness who, like Cecilia, was abandoned by a lover. Through various (and absurdly coincidental) plot twists, a stranger named Fernando arrives and is discovered to be Cecilia's husband and Stella's lover. The women express contradictory notions of passion and ambivalence regarding their errant spouse-lover, Fernando, who is stunned by the unexpected encounter with his wife and mistress, as well as a grown daughter he only remembers as a child, leading to fits of conscience and, ultimately, to suicide.

Adding a theatrical frame, Kushner makes use of some of Goethe's little-used secondary characters, including the town's postmistress and a steward in her inn to serve as narrative observers, pulling Goethe's pseudorealistic drama toward a more self-consciously theatrical style. Using elements from both the 1776 and 1806 versions, Kushner tweaks phrases, particularly those with comic potential, toward a more contemporary sensibility. Lucy, for example, comments on a handsome coachman in a straight translation from Goethe: "We had a happy, good looking young postilion. I'd like to travel all over the world with him,"[3] but Kushner changes this to have Lucy describe him as "very attractive. He could take me anywhere."[4] Kushner also brings *Stella*'s poignant qualities to the fore, as when Lucy recalls to her mother her feelings about Fernando's abandonment, "sitting on the little bed in the green room, crying because you cried" (I.5), or when the postmistress marvels at how "someone so unhappy can still manage to be so friendly and good" (I.8), describing Stella. In Kushner's hands *Stella* becomes a meditation on surviving loss, a theme running through *A Bright Room Called Day, Angels in America, Slavs!*, and *Caroline, or Change,* in which all characters either have experienced loss or will do so before the play ends. Kushner's juxtaposing of two endings (taken, in part, from Goethe's two versions) allows him to move beyond a mere exploration of the sufferings of love and to raise notions of love outside bourgeois expectations, undoubtedly an intriguing angle for a gay author. Kushner intends through this double ending to bring a relatively obscure play closer to a contemporary audience.

Kushner's adaptation of Heinrich von Kleist's 1810 short story *St. Cecilia, or The Power of Music,* was completed in 1997 as an operatic libretto. Kleist's story of four antireligious brothers who attack a convent in Aachen during festival time is set at the end of the sixteenth century. As the attack begins, the brothers are overwhelmed by music emanating from inside the cloister walls and are subsequently converted to Catholicism. Although Kleist's story would seem to demonstrate the positive impact of religion, the brothers become oddly dehumanized by their conversion, after which they are confined to an asylum. Dressed as monks and singing in eerie voices, they are at silent prayer before a crucifix when their mother arrives. Setting about to learn the reasons for their fate, she interviews a nun present on the day of the attack and learns that another nun, who was supposed to conduct the service, was taken ill and no one present knows for certain who actually conducted the music. The nuns consider it an act of God, believing he intervened to save their cloister from destruction.

Goethe complained of disturbing qualities in the often-grotesque and surreal elements of Kleist's work, as well as its psychological probings, but Kushner seems to have found in Kleist a writer struggling toward modern concerns whose sensitive examination of the inner workings of the mind, and his sideways glance at religious faith, exposes the power and incomprehensibility of spiritual belief. Ambivalent about his own faith, Kushner raises issues about various belief systems throughout his plays, from his beginnings as a dramatist, through his adaptation of the Yiddish classic *The Dybbuk,* and in *Hydriotaphia, Angels in America,* and this Kleist-inspired libretto.

Freely adapting Kleist's story while holding to the basic elements of its plot and characters, Kushner historicizes *St. Cecilia* with reflections on social questions of its era, particularly in regard to the rise of commerce and political activism. The intersections of art, commerce, and politics are examined within the

period Kleist sets the story, while Kushner makes pertinent connections to present-day social and religious tensions. His libretto
features a Brechtian structure of short, episodic scenes framing
the political musings typical of Kushner's own plays. The language is lyrical, but there is an uneasy atmosphere of social flux,
as in the opening scene outside a prison where three incarcerated
prostitutes set a grim mood: "On the wing the hungry owl; /
There is murder in the wind, / And the wolf is on the prowl / And
odor in the air."[5] This ominous lyric—reminiscent of the nightmarish speeches of Die Alte in *A Bright Room Called Day*—
emanates throughout *Hydriotaphia* and certain passages of
Angels in America, and in St. Cecelia it is set against volatile
local disagreements among merchants, intellectuals, workers,
and the nuns of the convent of St. Cecilia. The brothers, divided
in allegiances to these groups, are at odds over the attack. The
youngest brother cannot conceive that God does not reside in
such a holy place, while the others are inclined to drive out the
nuns, who they call "a shaved-headed lute-picking gaggle of
whores" (II.i.70). Sister Antonia, the ailing nun in charge of
music, insists on conducting mass despite her illness and the riot,
which leads to the death of a nun by stoning. At the same time
the eldest brother considers the mob's hatred of the nuns mis-
placed, insisting that the merchant class should be mistrusted
instead, noting that most of the nuns "come to the cloister to
escape the factory. / That's not divinity. That's not theology. /
That's not a mystery. That's only . . . History" (I.ii.88). In this
sense the Brechtian influence is centrally evident; Kushner
describes Brecht as "one of the great exemplars of what social
commitment in the theatre is about,"[6] and his faithful adaptations of Brecht's plays are instructive in revealing Kushner's
understanding of those elements of Brecht's aesthetics and political engagement guiding his own work.

Brecht, however, is not the only political dramatist Kushner has adapted. His brief collaboration on *Widows* with Ariel Dorfman, a Chilean author best known for the play *Death and the Maiden,* is a case in point. While struggling to make his novel *Widows* stage worthy, Dorfman invited Kushner to try. Set during the Pinochet dictatorship in Chile, *Widows* depicts the stubborn, courageous struggle of Sophia Fuentes, a peasant woman whose father, husband, and sons are abducted. As the play begins, they have become what the Chileans grimly referred to as "the disappeared." "Can you smell my breath? I've spent the last five hours talking to the dead,"[7] Sofia asks her neighbors as she communes with her lost men in a solitary struggle to give them rest by securing justice in Kushner's version. Underscoring the activism of a woman who refuses to forget her lost family, Kushner stresses the risks she takes to demand answers from the living. When the nearby river yields up a man's grossly disfigured body, Sofia insists it is her missing father. When another body appears, Sofia claims it as her husband. The women of her village follow Sofia's lead, asserting the moral significance of identifying unidentifiable corpses and honoring them. Authorities first dismiss the women's mournful dissidence until the political impact becomes evident. Sofia will settle for nothing less than the return of the men—dead or alive—and punishment for those who abducted and killed them. In Kushner's version Sofia is a moral lightning rod not unlike Agnes of *A Bright Room Called Day,* Prior of *Angels in America,* and Caroline Thibodeaux of *Caroline, or Change,* characters who represent the moral imperatives of troubled times. Sofia may be the most activist figure of all, risking her life and what little she has left to honor those she has lost.

Kushner's version of Dorfman's play features a Brechtian episodic structure and a stringent balancing of political and personal issues in the lives of the characters, underscoring the harrowing bravery inherent in Sofia's resistance and that of the peasant women who follow her. Sofia's actions are clearly more provocative in Kushner's version than in Dorfman's solo attempts at dramatizing the play, as he uses the women to provide a choric threnody of grief as in classical tragedy. Kushner commemorates the dead, as he did with AIDS sufferers in *Angels in America,* while also presenting a realistic account of atrocities committed under Pinochet, concluding his adaptation with the unarmed village women facing down the guns of soldiers intending to terminate their civil disobedience.

The simple religious faith of Sofia's community is brought to the center of Kushner's version of *Widows,* and, as with his own work, faith becomes a metaphor. Sofia explains the significance of the figure on her crucifix: "He writhes again on the cross, in pain again, He suffers His agonies, this frail young man, hoping to relieve the suffering of the world. But. There was too much suffering, too much sin. So his agonies never end."[8] Employing this and other archetypal symbols—a magical blue chair, the river, the disfigured bodies of the dead—and linguistic metaphors, such as referring to children as seed corn, Kushner converts ordinary aspects of Chilean village life into iconic imagery. Dorfman and Kushner worked on a subsequent version of the script, and Dorfman made additional changes after Kushner relinquished involvement. Critical response was mixed when the final version opened at the Mark Taper Forum in 1991. The play's representation of the unrepresented and the political ramifications of governmental corruption, here shown in especially brutal form, undoubtedly drew Kushner to *Widows,* which echoes the concerns of his own plays.

In the mid-1990s Kushner looked, somewhat improbably, to the fairy tales of the Brothers Grimm, adapting "The Two Journeymen" as an unproduced screenplay, *Grim(m)*. The title is an obvious word play with its second *m* as a reminder of the source of the story, while the single *m* variant establishes mood. Kushner's central character, Amanda, a bright, young, African American schoolteacher in the present-day Bronx, tries to help poverty-stricken minority students who are further disadvantaged by inequities in the school budget and, as Kushner asserts, will be further harmed when New Gingrich's "Contract with America" prevails. For Amanda (speaking for Kushner) the Contract with America is a confirmation of discrimination "against the poor, the sick and the elderly."[9]

Amanda reads "The Two Journeymen" to her class, pointing out a lesson drawn from its title. A journeyman, she explains, is someone "trying to learn to do something special, like all of you," and in Gingrich's America, it means making "do with less than you need" (7). Amanda experiences disturbing dreams of herself on a desert, a nightmare scene that Kushner allows to slowly bleed into the bleak urban reality Amanda faces daily. The fairy tale increasingly dominates her subconscious; in dreams she encounters a frail, old man known only as The Man, once prosperous and now a migrant. He accuses Amanda of not paying attention to what is happening around her, insisting that "you are living in the past, someone will take care of you *you think, you assume* and now you're probably going to die. And nowadays no one will come by to pick up your carcass, like before, some tax-paid carcass-picker-upper sent 'round to salvage the remains of morons who can't be bothered to stay *informed*" (11). Interweaving Amanda's dream with elements of the Grimm fairy tale to underscore present sociopolitical issues, Kushner breaks away from the episodic structure he typically employs to allow the story to flow cinematically from dreams to reality.

As Amanda's dream darkens and as the socioeconomic disasters resulting from Gingrich's policies deepen at her school, she abandons her class and hustles to a subway. Finding herself near Brooklyn's Gowanus Canal, Amanda discovers a beautiful garden in the midst of an otherwise devastated neighborhood. Annie, an elderly woman, invites Amanda into the garden that was created by neighbors despite apathy from local government. Discussing "The Two Journeymen," Annie posits that the behavior of The Man, like that of Gingrich's political allies, is explained by the fact that "the Wicked don't like their victims, and they don't like witnesses" (37). At this point an injured student appears (a haunting figure reminiscent of Vodya, the little Russian girl dying of radiation in *Slavs!*), and Amanda wonders what happened to the resources intended to help those in need. The little girl points to a covered bucket that, when turned over, reveals gold coins instantly transformed into bumblebees. Kushner ends the screenplay with another transformation, with Amanda's voice heard reading: "The hills and valleys are far apart and never do they meet, but the children of God oftentimes do, and sometimes the Good meet with the Bad" (39), as a bee walks across the word "GRIMM," shown in old German Gothic letters on the book's cover, and the type abruptly transforms to reveal the word "GRIM" in modern print. Amanda, like many of Kushner's women characters, including Agnes in *A Bright Room Called Day*, Dame Dorothy in *Hydriotaphia*, Harper in *Angels in America*, and Bonfila and Katherina in *Slavs!*, finds herself living through social and personal disasters beyond her control. In a collision of dreams, hallucinations, and visions, these women survive by either hunkering down until the storm of social disaster passes over them or by rising up as activist spirits. If hope is not possible, as seems to be the case for Amanda, Kushner calls for locating a survival strategy, creating something like Annie's garden (a vision from Voltaire), where imagining a better future is possible.

The economic and social woes evident in *Grim(m)* are also the crux of Kushner's adaptations of Brecht's plays. In *The Good Person of Setzuan*, Brecht's 1940 play adapted by Kushner and first performed at San Diego's La Jolla Playhouse in 1994 (followed by a Wings Theatre Company production off Broadway in 1999), an examination of the battle for the survival of the human soul in a cruel, mercenary world continues. Existential questions of faith are at the heart of *St. Cecilia* and surface at the center of Kushner's Brecht adaptations, but the harsh universe Brecht's characters find themselves living in stems, in part, from the economic and political construction of society, a concern Kushner highlights in his faithful adaptation. Marxist critic Raymond Williams, another major influence on Kushner, writes of Brecht's attentiveness to themes of "the individual against society,"[10] and this concept is central in *The Good Person of Setzuan*, a fable concerning attempts by a Chinese woman to live a moral life while trapped in abject poverty in a corrupt society. Through the simplicity of an episodic parable, themes unfold in layers, with increasingly complex (and contradictory) historical and cultural meanings arising. Liberated from the constraints of either realistic illusion or three-dimensional characters, the play's episodes exploit variations of a few overarching themes, an approach prized by Kushner, who adds his own cinematic sensibility to Brecht's structure, overlapping episodes as in his own plays. Brecht's use of fable to recount (and reevaluate) human history alienates his audience from distracting details of contemporary reality even as the story reflects upon them. Kushner draws his characters closer to his audience through his allegiance to American lyric realism, while also adopting Brecht's insistence that the theater's mode of representation must come second to what is represented. The play's thematic concerns are bound up with political notions; in other words *The Good Person of Setzuan*'s emphasis rests on the relationship of the individual to the construction of society. Kushner largely eschews Brecht's distancing techniques regarding character—his characters are more fully drawn and distinctly individual, more emotionally drawn, and although they may step out of the "reality" of their world, they are real people, not icons serving as thematic mouthpieces, as is typical of Brecht (although they may serve this function at times). This critical difference between Brecht and Kushner has an impact in Kushner's adaptations of Brecht, although both playwrights share a sense of the changeable nature of situations, individuals, and societies as deeply political and, at the same time, fundamentally dramatic.

The paradoxical nature of humans is taken to its extreme in *The Good Person of Setzuan* as Brecht's protagonist, the good-hearted Chinese prostitute Shen Te, invents an alter ego, Shui Ta, to guard (or supersede) her instinctively generous and compassionate spirit. Shui Ta's avaricious, self-absorbed nature protects Shen Te, providing a defense against the overwhelming tests of morality and compassion she faces. Brecht and Kushner are bound together in their belief that the exclusive province of the stage is to create such contradictions as a means of releasing both human nature and the inherent social questions shaping human experience. Kushner approaches *The Good Person of*

Setzuan as a parable, or "agrarian folk poetry,"[11] with a central character who must not fall into "essentialism, she must not be 'essentially' good."[12] Kushner's version of Brecht's statement of Shen Te's dilemma is spoken to the gods by the character herself:

> Your first decree
> To be good and to live
> Split me, like lightning, in two. I
> Don't know how it happened: to be good to others
> And to myself was not possible for me,
> To help others, and myself, was too hard.
> Ah, your world is hard. Too much need, too much despair![13]

Kushner contends that this speech is "the most obvious, corny thing in the world, and it is also immensely powerful,"[14] a significant statement explaining the enduring potency of Brecht's drama and what it inspires in politically engaged dramatists like Kushner. His simple directness, combined with Kushner's more deeply psychological rendering of Shen Te's suffering, serve as a call to arms; in short it is the essence of political theater.

Kushner's reverence for Brecht emerged in his early play *The Heavenly Theatre*, which he describes as concerning "this extraordinary historical phenomenon of a revolution that takes place during a carnival" and notes that it was his attempt to understand "Brechtian dramaturgy"[15] and to establish an approach permitting him to construct his own variation on it. Kushner's first play in the Brechtian mode was undoubtedly *A Bright Room Called Day*, written as a response to—or argument with—Brecht's *Fear and Misery of the Third Reich*, a play similar to *A Bright Room Called Day* in its examination of the impact of Hitler's rise on ordinary Germans through a fusing of personal and political concerns. Kushner's drama, like Brecht's, is inextricably bound to the problems of a capitalist society. *The Good Person of Setzuan* employs Marxist concepts to depict the inequities inherent in capitalism and to pose variant political views within a capitalist society. Locating countertheories—or finding strategies for those disenfranchised by capitalism—are within Kushner's conception of Brecht's play. Kushner is inexorably influenced by the triumph of capitalism in American society (and the world in the aftermath of the collapse of the Soviet Union), a reality "where people who are white have money and people who aren't white are frequently struggling economically. I think that the way that race and poverty are frequently conjoined work very well for this play,"[16] as they also function in *Caroline, or Change,* which confronts economic inequity directly within its own cultural idiom. Despite the national change of venue with *The Good Person of Setzuan,* Kushner points up the dilemma that "something is terribly wrong in the world. Goodness is punished severely and wickedness is the only way to survive. What is that? The great villain is an economic system which creates terrible deprivation and want."[17]

The terrible deprivation and want of the world in which Shen Te lives parallel those of the contemporary world and result not so much from a "collapse of morality,"[18] as millennial neoconservative politicians would have it, but from the economic and racial inequities of capitalism. These inequities are all evident in the deprivations of Shen Te's world, which are meant to reflect those in Brecht's own time; Kushner in turn subtly relates them to the inequities of the present-day American economy. The times of Shen Te and Brecht are distinct historical periods offering Kushner opportunities to relate questions about the ways in which a small, privileged class prospers while the remainder of society seems perpetually to slide further down the economic scale. Linking Brecht's play to American economic and social concerns, Kushner is at his most Brechtian. Stopping short of a call for class warfare, he questions the ways in which the disenfranchised suffer in any time and place, most particularly the present. Cultural clashes between rich and poor and conceptions about how individuals at the opposite ends of the economic spectrum experience good and evil are present in Brecht's *The Good Person of Setzuan*, as well as in Kushner's adaptation where the moral issues—both personal and societal—are emphasized, with Kushner noting that "what makes me crazy is that nobody can talk about economics anymore. Nobody can talk about capitalism. Nobody can talk about the notion that workers have rights, or that maybe the rich aren't entitled to maximize profit to the moon and have no regard for human life or the environment or jobs. Maybe downsizing is immoral. Maybe these things need to be looked at again."[19]

By emphasizing economic questions (and without eliminating anything of significance from Brecht's original text), Kushner stresses the sociopolitical issues in *The Good Person of Setzuan*, underscoring resonances to the contemporary world and striving to humanize Brecht's iconic characters. His contributions are most evident in his adaptation of Brecht's lyrics, which he has more overtly support the play's thematic core. His bare-bones approach permits meaning to emerge without unnecessary elaborations or a too-literal approach. Kushner's writing style is by nature more voluptuous than Brecht's, yet he restrains himself to serve Brecht, as demonstrated when Shen Te speaks for poor children by imagining her own: "What kind of world / Are you coming to? Will you too / Be an ashcan scavenger?" (133). She proposes that the child become a tiger in responding to the world: "Everything I've learned / In the gutter-school of my life,

/ Fighting and betraying, now / It will serve you, my son, to you / I will be good, a tiger, a wild animal / To all others, if that's how it has to be. And / It must be" (133). Asserting the play's central precept and the character's dilemma, Kushner molds Brecht's lyrics to add realism to Shen Te's cry of determined despair and to the motivation for her alter ego. Here Kushner joins with Brecht, challenging audiences to reckon with this unanswerable plea.

Kushner's other changes to Brecht's language come in the exchange of one set of colloquialisms for another, more contemporary variety. Kushner finds that the "syncopation and brusqueness of American English and its mongrel quality works well with Brecht, who goes quickly from [formal] German to something very short and choppy and nasal and street—the Berlin hip talk of the '20s and '30s,"[20] recognizing that there are distinct languages within the play that are important: the rural dialect spoken mostly by Shen Te and the "harsher language of business and the more sophisticated urban cultural rhetoric."[21] Colloquialisms distinguish characters by class, and Kushner emphasizes linguistic differences, deepening distinguishing personality traits Brecht employs to keep the characters archetypes as opposed to the fully dimensioned individuals Kushner prefers. Brecht's Shen Te is a delicate, full-hearted woman, exuding innate gentility, while steely qualities emerge in the persona of her alter ego, Shui Ta. Kushner merges the dual personas more fully, building empathy for a being faced with appallingly harsh choices. Shen Te soldiers on, as Kushner's text illuminates, with intellectual clarity on the complex dilemma she faces; as such, themes emerge directly through Shen Te's persona, with the result that the play's central questions come into full focus: is it possible to be moral and compassionate and to pursue personal happiness in a world of staggering need, corruption, and greed?

Kushner also brings his contemporary sensibility to bear on *The Good Person of Setzuan*'s secondary figures: the Gods, Wang the water seller, and especially the young pilot Yang Sun, a character at once pitiable and menacing. Kushner believes Brecht's characters "have a certain universality and fit very easily"[22] into a change of cultural idiom, permitting Brecht's dialogue to retain intended meaning while providing a more contemporary sound and language choices (not typical of standard Brecht translations). Accentuating the play's inherent ironic humor with a postmodern sensibility, Kushner refreshes the play through his restrained and precise adapting.

Kushner's most significant departure from Brecht, both in *The Good Person of Setzuan* and a subsequent adaptation of *Mother Courage and Her Children,* as well as in his own plays inspired by Brechtian techniques, is in empathetic characters. Brecht's vaunted technique of alienation requires him to view characters as cloaks worn by actors whose presence is openly asserted. Kushner's characters similarly break the theatrical fourth wall but always remain "in character" when they do so; the actor is not as evident as in Brecht. Kushner's dialogue maintains both stereotypical elements in the Brechtian sense, while adding dimensionality and emotional humanism typical of American drama. Adapting the play for a contemporary audience, Kushner's colloquialisms include obscenities and scatological elements. The dramaturgical alchemy merging Brecht and Williams is unique to Kushner's plays; it is most evident in *Angels in America* but is present in his other major plays.

Ultimately it is the use of the stage as a vehicle for sociopolitical debate that most closely links Kushner to Brecht. And both concur that in the case of Shen Te's aggrieved existence, an economic system prevails that "creates terrible deprivation and want" where "there isn't enough money and people don't have good houses and people don't have enough food, people don't have the luxury to develop their souls—people are crushed and tortured by acts of desperation." [23]

The depiction of desperation continues in Kushner's adaptation of Brecht's *Mother Courage and Her Children,* produced by the Public Theater in the summer of 2006 at the Delacorte Theater in New York's Central Park. Similarly springing from Kushner's reverence for Brecht and socialist political theory, Kushner finds a vehicle for expressing dismay with the Iraq War. The adaptation makes topical connections throughout, in part because Brecht's 1941 antiwar play fits virtually any period of armed conflict. In Kushner's estimation, *Mother Courage* describes "history as the accumulation of catastrophes and calamity," [24] an idea with particular resonance in a post-9/11 world. He considers *Mother Courage* "the greatest play written in the twentieth century," [25] a work, as one critic explains, that "pricks the conscience and challenges the system we think of as civilized society." [26] Brecht, Kushner believes, exudes "an absolutely serious desire to see the world change *now,* as they say in *Setzuan:* 'Now, Now, Now.' The urgency of that 'Now' is something that I go back to Brecht for." [27]

As the Iraq War dragged on into the summer of 2006, the antiwar immediacy of *Mother Courage* became obvious; the tragic destructiveness of war in any time is explored on myriad levels in Kushner's adaptation (as in Brecht's original play), with emphasis on history, on the human addiction to conflict, and on the economic forces propelling civilization toward war. As such, *Mother Courage* is also an anticapitalist play in which war is merely a welcome mercantile opportunity, a continuation of business by other means. *New York Times* critic Ben Brantley called Kushner's adaptation a "gallows vaudeville that has an all-too-reverberant relevance in these days of war,"[28] stressing those parallels Kushner finds between Brecht's play, set in the seventeenth century and reflecting the two world wars of the twentieth century through which Brecht lived (he lost a son in World War II), and the topical concerns of the present-day Iraq conflict. Critics reported on audience members bursting into spontaneous applause at certain lines, as when the cook states that "it's expensive, liberty, especially when you start exporting it to other countries"[29] or "he's always had principles, our king, and with his clear conscience he doesn't get depressed."[30] Keeping the adaptation in the period of the Thirty Years' War did not prevent Kushner from dropping in topical references without naming the contemporary names. The allusions were hard to miss, as when Mother Courage says, "It's when the general's a moron that the soldiers have to be brave."[31] Such lines are meant to incite anger as a precursor to active resistance in the most Brechtian sense. Rage can be paralyzing (as Kushner dramatized in Agnes's fear of the rising tide of Nazism in *A Bright Room Called Day*), but it can also inspire forceful action, as Mother Courage calls for in a conversation with a young soldier who has a momentary outburst: "It was short-lived anger, when what you needed was long-lasting rage."[32]

When *Mother Courage* premiered in Berlin in 1949, the impact of war and its devastations were still vividly with the German audiences. Despite the tragedies of 9/11 and the subsequent "war on terror" that had spread from Afghanistan to Iraq by 2006 and despite a mounting death toll in the increasingly unpopular war, Kushner's audience was less immersed in day-to-day realities of war. Stressing contemporary relevance, the problem of language emerged as central to Kushner, who pointed out that Brecht used a German dialect to create "an approximation of 17th-century German, not modern, sort of Bavarian, but with modern things in it. It's not like *The Good Person of Setzuan,* which is written in sort of a clean, plain style."[33] *Mother Courage* depends on what Kushner describes as a "rough and bumpy" language, "with a lot of commas and run-on sentences, and it's hard to find an American approximation for it."[34] Choosing a more conversational style, allowing a clarity and directness permitting the play's tragedy and humor to surface without excessive adornment, Kushner makes the cook's poverty humorous without a loss of the point, as when he explains to Mother Courage, "I'm not broke. I'm between money."[35] Kushner's intent to make the jokes more "ha-ha funny"[36] than in the original leads him to augment dialogue. He changes, for example, Mother Courage's statement about her mute daughter, Kattrin, which in Eric Bentley's standard translation reads as "she's not a captivating young person, she's a respectable young person," to "she isn't comely, she's stay-at-homely, and I don't want clergy sniffing up my daughter."[37] Similarly Kushner has Mother Courage refer to her half-Finnish son, Eilif, as a "brazen stickyfingered fork-tongued son of a Finn," while in Bentley's Brecht he is merely a "Finnish devil."[38] Such liberties disturb literalists, yet such choices permit Kushner to disinter meaning and ensure that the play functions as living theater. Despite the fact that he considers his more explicit treatment of Brecht's implicit references as essentially faithful, Kushner's version is truly a free adaptation.

Critics remarked favorably on Meryl Streep's performance (although several felt she was miscast), noting her skill at nodding to Brechtian alienation without being bound by it. Allowing the character's vulnerability to show through without losing allegorical resonance was accomplished by the humanizing touches Kushner brought to the text, techniques similar to those he had applied to Shen Te in *The Good Person of Setzuan*. He appropriately shapes the adaptation around Mother Courage, a tough, shrewd woman who emerges as a small icon of the excesses of capitalism, a "battlefield hyena,"[39] cynical, self-absorbed, and swaggering through the most bruising lessons of life and war, learning in the process to repress empathy for the suffering of others to survive. As Mother Courage says of her ill-fated daughter, Kattrin, "She suffers because she pities."[40] Abandoning pity by the side of the road as she journeys through a world on fire, Mother Courage is simultaneously heroic, foolish, and malign, embodying the earth mother and the social parasite, exploiter and exploited. Spouting folk philosophies of a most practical nature, Mother Courage reflects the thematic yin and yang of the play, at once detached and engaged, cynical and passionate, ironic and vulnerable. The implicit ironies embedded in these contradictions are made explicit by Kushner, whose dialogue and verses frame the conception that an individual's admirable qualities are liabilities in the insanity of war, as when gentle Kattrin, performing the play's sole truly heroic act, is shot to death warning an unsuspecting town of a forthcoming siege. Mother Courage saves her skin if not her soul through greed and wit, while the perversity of wartime morality is illuminated when Eilif becomes a hero for stealing a farmer's stock to feed a general, a criminal act in peacetime. A similar moral reversal occurs when the hapless chaplain's faith-based oratory is twisted in service of encouraging conscripts to fight to their deaths. These hypocrisies and calumnies provide the only consistency in a chaotic play that finds its strength as the inconsistencies pile up in episodic and repetitive sequences, in differing moods. Kushner's rough language supports Brecht's notion that no one emerges unscathed, physically or morally, from war. In Kushner's adaptation, Mother Courage states a wrenching paradox: she prefers war to peacetime when, she insists, want and injustices are more severely felt by the masses.

Kushner's adaptation is epic in scope, exploiting and extending the most didactic characteristics of Brecht's text. The overarching theme of war's cost, which in the case of Mother Courage entails the loss of her three children, one after another, is absurdly ironic. She loses everything that matters for the sin of profiting from war, a terrible penance intended to engender both sympathy and antipathy for her. Like Amanda in *Grim(m)*, Mother Courage indomitably journeys forth to confront forces of politics, economics, and human desire (and need) beyond her control (or full understanding), and in compromising (or abandoning) morality to survive, she becomes a haunting figure, a conniving specter representing the degradations of war and its crushing human costs. In Kushner's acrid reconfiguring of Brecht, Mother Courage states this directly: "What works out best for us is what they call paralysis, a shot here, one step forward, one step back."[41] The suggestion of paralysis as the winds of change blow through the world connects Kushner's conception of this Brecht character with his own characters, particularly Agnes of *A Bright Room Called Day*, a woman lacking the resourcefulness of Mother Courage, yet understanding that the only option is mere survival. Left alone to live out an empty survival in which it is business as usual, Mother Courage, like Samuel Beckett's existential tramps in *Waiting for Godot*, haunts modern drama in a war-riddled century. Prior and Harper in *Angels in America* are similarly iconic survivors battered by forces beyond their control; the fierce stasis of Caroline Thibodeaux of *Caroline, or Change* and the resigned hopelessness of Amanda in *Grim(m)* are also variations on this theme.

The *New Yorker*'s Hilton Als called Kushner's adaptation "brilliant,"[42] and most critics were positive although mixed on whether colloquialisms and relating the text to current events helped or hindered. Eric Bentley's standard translation of *Mother Courage* was generally found wanting in comparison with Kushner's treatment, which retained core meanings of Brecht's language without becoming unnecessarily literal. Kushner's emphasis on loss and suffering, recurrent themes in his own plays, is emphasized in his Brecht adaptation, as when Mother Courage encounters a complaining soldier. She makes clear that he has yet to truly understand suffering; at this point Kushner's lyrics are poignantly direct: "Birdsong up above: / Push comes to shove. / Soon you fall down from the grandstand. . . . / And then: it's all downhill. / Your fall was God's will."[43]

Questions of God's will and especially the idea that God is not necessarily a benign force are present in many Kushner plays, most obviously in *Angels in America,* where an errant, unseen God disappears to parts unknown, leaving humanity to fend for itself during the disastrous twentieth century. The international tragedies of the modern world are seen in embryonic form in perhaps Kushner's most informative adaptation, *A Dybbuk,* freely adapted in 1994 from S. Ansky's Yiddish theater chestnut, *The Dybbuk.* Produced first by the Hartford Stage Company that year, followed by a New York Public Theater production in 1997, Kushner worked from Joachim Neugroschel's literal translation retitled *A Dybbuk, or Between Two Worlds.* This free adaptation reveals Kushner's recurrent concerns with the joys and heartbreaks of love, his sense of the impact of sweeping sociopolitical and economic realities on individual lives, and, most centrally, a religious skepticism that is coupled with a deep yearning for faith and poised on a philosophical fissure between modernist and postmodernist thought.

As with *The Illusion,* Kushner finds in Ansky's play opportunities to enhance its inherent theatricality and passionate emotionalism, while engaging in a Talmudic questioning of the natures of love and faith, and their intersections. Images of past Jewish life and the rigidly orthodox belief system in Eastern European shtetlach depicted by Ansky allow Kushner to experiment with conjunctions of these images of the past and contemporary anxieties, as he had done with Brecht's plays. Kushner takes many more liberties with Ansky, and his adaptation is, in essence, an exploration of his own ambivalence about religion. Among Kushner's prior works, a forerunner to *A Dybbuk* can be found in a one-act piece, *"It's an Undoing World," or Why Should It Be Easy When It Can Be Hard? Notes on My Grandma for Actors, Dancers and a Band,* in which Kushner experiments with techniques of mystical fantasy and themes similar to those in *A Dybbuk* on a smaller, more personal (and pseudoautobiographical) scale, demonstrating what Harold Bloom calls his "authentic gift for fantasy."[44] In this one act, disembodied spirits live in a family heirloom teapot—"Oooooooyyyyyyyy . . . It's an undoing world, I'm telling you,"[45] wails one—daughters find comfort sleeping on their father's graves, and knowledge is passed through the hands of men and women as they dance. Old World traditions merge with present-day struggles in the experiences of an elderly woman not unlike Sarah Ironson, Louis's deceased grandmother in *Angels in America,* who has lived in both worlds and, in her senility, confuses memories of the two, rearranging history to reveal the trials and contradictions in the lives of the generation of immigrants who shaped twentieth-century America with those experiences that shaped them in the Old World.

That Old World is center stage in the comparatively simple plot Kushner carries over from Ansky's play. Often referred to as a Yiddish *Romeo and Juliet, A Dybbuk* recounts a tragic romance between Chonen, a young rabbinical student, and Leah, daughter of Reb Sender, a well-to-do merchant. Sender made a pact with Chonen's long-dead father that Chonen and Leah would one day marry, yet despite this he breaks the pact and promises Leah to another young man whose family will bring financial opportunities. Chonen dies in despair over this betrayal, returning as a malevolent spirit—a dybbuk—possessing Leah's body. Sender sends for Rabbi Azriel, an exorcist, in hopes of freeing Leah from the dybbuk's hold. After an epic struggle, Azriel succeeds at the cost of Leah's life, and the lovers, destined to be together, are united in another world (Ansky, an ethnographer, learned of an actual incident in a small town where a monument was erected to a bride and groom killed on their wedding day in the eighteenth century). Kushner maintains Ansky's basic plot and archetypal characters, introducing more dimensions to them, adding a complicated sexuality, and stressing parallels between Old World traditions and the dawning of modernity. Ansky's play, written circa 1912–14 as modernist thought, widespread immigration, and technological developments hastened the disappearance of traditional Eastern European Jewish life, is carried further by Kushner, who adds allusions to the coming Holocaust, the profound impact of technological progress, and the resultant religious skepticism springing from both.

Kushner's most significant embellishment is the introduction of skepticism in the character of Rabbi Azriel, whose own faith is shown to be deeply shaken by the multiple tragedies of the world and, in particular, the agonies of Chonen and Leah. Ansky's rabbi is a one-dimensional man of faith; by introducing ambivalence to the character, Kushner reveals his mistrust of patriarchal tendencies in Judaism and, in fact, of most ancient religions. As a homosexual, Kushner condemns the long history of homophobia in religious tradition by imbuing *A Dybbuk* with both homoeroticism, as when rabbinical students indulge in an orgiastic dance, and the conventional romantic passions of Chonen and Leah. Alicia Solomon identifies *A Dybbuk's* "intensely homosocial world" that "vibrates with erotic implication,"[46] supplying the play with an intricate undercurrent of sensuality. Enhancing this, Kushner's Chonen delivers a passionate recitation of the "Song of Songs" for Leah while stressing that Chonen, as the dybbuk, penetrates Leah's body in a complex merger of spirituality and sexuality.

Kushner considers that a hint of religious doubt is evident in Ansky's *The Dybbuk* in the depiction of "a very insular, premodern shtetl world, but one that's already being impacted upon by modernity and the arrival of the nineteenth century, and everything that would come after that."[47] He imagines Ansky's skepticism and the impact of European political upheavals emerging in that period as central to the play's continued viability, suggesting that Ansky "went toward Judaism by his political convictions" and that his "sense of himself as a political revolutionary was very much at odds with this sort of emotional tie that he had with Judaism," which Ansky described as the sole motif of his drama: "spiritual struggle."[48] The intense intellectual debates on social and spiritual issues combine with fevered flights of fantasy in Kushner's adaptation as in his own plays. He grapples with social circumstances, the cultural and religious heritage of his characters, and their contradictory emotions and desires, particularly regarding love and faith. *A Dybbuk,* like Kushner's other plays, evokes an anxious and troubled humanism.

Kushner substantially restructures Ansky's text into a Brecht-ian episodic framework as in his early original plays from *A Bright Room Called Day* to *Slavs!*, a structure he moves away from, or significantly modifies, in the more cinematic *Home-body/Kabul* and *Caroline, or Change*. He brings to *A Dybbuk* the guarded optimism of his major plays, tempered by postmod-ern doubt. Hope springs from the lessons learned from loss Kushner stresses in his own plays, and in *A Dybbuk* he plays up those qualities of Ansky's text. Chonen is unable to bear the loss of Leah in this world, yet wins her in the next. Wrongs may ulti-mately be righted, Kushner implies, the universe may be put in order, although not in expected ways. The significance of the adaptation's subtitle, *Between Two Worlds,* springs from a range of dualities, as Alisa Solomon explains: "Death resides in life, male in female, the spiritual in the carnal, religious doubt in devotion, evil in goodness, social well-being in private acts, Hasidism in modernity, the holy in the profane. And, in each instance, vice versa."[49] And, it might reasonably be added, real life in fantasy. Kushner employs these dualities to probe ancient Judaic religious and secular traditions that reflect on the impact of the spiritual and natural worlds on the intimate lives of in-dividuals. And in his own plays, particularly *A Bright Room Called Day, Angels in America, Slavs!,* and his adaptation of *Widows,* Kushner communes with the dead, considering the pos-sibility of relationships that continue past the grave and of ulti-mate justice, if not in this world, perhaps in the next.

Kushner adds and eliminates dialogue, abandons antiquated theatrical devices, and draws out universal significances to refresh aesthetic power and emotional force. As previously sug-gested, the adaptation shifts focus from the romantic tragedy of Chonen and Leah to Azriel's theological skepticism. He adds a speech permitting Azriel to agonize over his crisis of faith when, alone with his scribe, he cries out to his deceased grandfather of a world grown wicked, of scientific change, and of pogroms. The people "don't pray. I'm older than my years, I don't sleep at night. Under my robe, my knees knock together in fear sometimes. (Softly) And sometimes, Grandfather, I do not entirely trust God. (To the Scribe) Don't write that down."[50] Azriel's despair, the apocalyptic anxiousness of a troubled century, is played out in a little Jewish shtetl, a world in which God has either turned away from humanity or become malevolent.

Kushner foreshadows the coming horrors of the Holocaust that finally obliterates the Old World Azriel feels slowly slipping away—most obviously in the onstage arrival of Azriel in a railroad boxcar, a visual reminder of the forced transportation of Jews to Nazi concentration camps. Kushner highlights this imagery by adding the telling line: "In a world of electric light, even Jews can ride the trains" (66). More overtly he offers a scene in which Azriel's scribe records the exorcism and is stunned when an unseen hand fills a blank page with a description of the unimaginable horrors Jews will face only decades hence: "At some not-very-distant date / the martyred dead accumulate; / books of history will contain / mountain-piles of the slain" (101). Embellishing Ansky's text with lyrical touches, Kushner describes Torah scrolls as "dark men engulfed in shadows, draped in velvet shawls, bent over mysteries" (21) and makes use of the time period and ethnic specificity of Ansky's play to bring out the social, historical, and sexual connotations of dybbuk folklore. At the same time Kushner's contemporary awareness negotiates an uneasy truce between fundamental religious faith (and mysticism) and the secular (and real) world. His focus on the historical ravages of the past, the fearfulness of a future without traditional faiths, individual human longing for atonement and spiritual redemption, and on honoring the dead and cherishing the living are intended to transform a dramatic curio into vital drama.

Kushner stretches the play's stylistic boundaries, maintaining its qualities as a supernatural folktale of crossed worlds, hearts, and historical ages, while reckoning with its orthodox religious ritual and, most important, its depictions of unformed and unutterable longings beyond human governance. Claims of the dead on the living, the merging of the worlds of both (demonic possession is, in fact, a passion carried beyond life into the realm of death), and the relationship of Jews to each other and to God shatter narrow definitions of gender and history. In the final scene Kushner has Azriel send a pointed message to God: "Though His love become only abrasion, derision, excoriation, tell Him, I cling. We cling. He made us, He can never shake us off. We will always find Him out. Promise Him that. We will always find Him, no matter how few there are, tell Him we will find Him. To deliver our complaint" (106). This speech echoes Prior's determination in *Angels in America*, the demand for more life from an angelic council.

Kushner's interest in East European Judaic traditions continues to be manifested in his work, from a small, two-character one-act piece, *Notes on Akiba*, which he himself performed with theater director Michael Mayer, to his stated plan to adapt another Yiddish classic, *The Golem*. This enduring tale deals with the old myth of a golem created as protector of the Jews, a distinctly urban play, as opposed to the rural environment of *A Dybbuk*. Acknowledging the historical oppression of the Jews in these plays, Kushner focuses attention on how to "confront anti-Semitism . . . How do you confront the genocidal intent of the world without yourself becoming a murderer, and without usurping certain things which are proscribed by God?"[51]—a theme that would recur in his screenplay *Munich*. Depicting the Israeli hit squad formed to avenge the killing of Israel's athletes at the 1972 Munich Olympics, *Munich* is typically Kushnerian in its exploration of the moral costs of revenge, even when it can be justified and, as important, with the ongoing threats to the oppressed, like Jews, who most deeply feel apocalyptic anxiety in the postmodern world.

CHAPTER 7

Screenplays and Other Writings

For a decade beginning with the appearance of *Angels in America* in the early 1990s, Tony Kushner's success as a playwright paralleled a frustrating encounter with the movie business. His sudden success led to an offer to script the live-action movie *The Flintstones,* while more suitable projects did not come to fruition. As early as 1990 Universal Pictures optioned *The Illusion,* Kushner's Corneille adaptation, and in 1995 he was announced as the screenwriter for *The Mayor of Castro Street,* a film about the life of Harvey Milk starring Dustin Hoffman, but neither film was produced. Similarly the possibility of an *Angels in America* film languished, not least because the two-part, seven-hour epic seemed too long for a single movie. Producers balked at making two films, although legendary director Robert Altman, whose 1975 screen classic *Nashville* had partly inspired the structure of *Angels in America,* worked with Kushner on plans for a two-film treatment before deciding the project was too problematic. Other directors were announced after Altman's withdrawal, but no screen version of *Angels in America* appeared during the 1990s.

In the interim new Kushner plays were produced, including *Slavs!, Homebody/Kabul,* and *Caroline, or Change,* as well as two as-yet-unfinished projects, *The Intelligent Homosexual's Guide to Capitalism and Socialism, with a Key to the Scriptures* and *Henry Box Brown, or The Mirror of Slavery.* The latter is intended as part of a trilogy on economic history that Kushner describes as "about the relationship between the textile industry in Britain and American slavery that has a more conventionally epic form"[1] in the Brechtian tradition. It was announced for production at the Royal National Theatre of Great Britain. In this piece Kushner weaves together history, personal lives, and his progressive politics centered around the historic figure of Henry Brown, a former slave and, later, a critic of economic policies encouraging slavery. Brown escaped bondage in 1849 by shipping himself in a canvas-lined crate from Virginia to Philadelphia, and his extraordinary escape was widely covered in the media, leading him to write an autobiography, *Narrative of the Life of Henry Box Brown, Written by Himself,* a title acknowledging the addition to his name of "Box" as a commemoration of his odd mode of transportation to freedom. The first English edition of the book began with a simple verse, "Forget not the unhappy," a line Kushner uses to frame themes regarding the oppressions and moral conundrums of nineteenth-century capitalism. Kushner told the *New York Times* that he is "drawn to writing historical characters. The best stories are the ones you find in history,"[2] and much of his full-scale work is similarly sweeping in scale, theme, characterization, and language. He describes the play as concerning itself with the English textile industry and its connection to the institution of slavery in pre–Civil War America centered on "the international character of capital" and its impact on slavery, "a bizarre holdover from earlier social formations," which "was primarily bankrolled by a foreign country in the interest of supporting an empire. I'm interested in the question of the internationalist solidarity of labor: I think a very good case can be made that the British working class is essentially what kept Britain out of our Civil War."[3] While *Henry Box Brown* remains a work in progress,

Kushner's *Caroline, or Change* pursued economic oppressions visited on African Americans in the 1960s and the historic linking of race and economics.

Kushner also wrote several one-act plays, including the aforementioned *It's an Undoing World, Notes on Akiba, G. David Schine in Hell,* and *Only We Who Guard the Mystery Shall Be Unhappy.* Two others, *Reverse Transcription* and *Terminating,* added new facets to long-standing Kushner themes. *Reverse Transcription: Six Playwrights Bury a Seventh; A Ten-Minute Play That's Nearly Twenty Minutes Long* was written in 1996 for the Humana New Play Festival at the Actors Theatre of Louisville, where Kushner directed the production himself (he has also staged plays as diverse as Clifford Odets's *Golden Boy* and Ellen McLaughlin's *Helen*). An amusing depiction of fictional playwrights based on writers Kushner knows, *Reverse Transcription* is set at Martha's Vineyard, where the playwrights are secretly burying an old playwright, Ding. While digging his grave, they unearth truths about themselves, the dangers and follies of life as dramatists, and the many meanings of their shared profession.

The six writers are an assortment of types, varied in ethnicity, sexual orientation, and levels of critical or commercial success: some are acclaimed, some are unknown; some rich, some struggling financially; some prolific, some not. The difficulty of developing six characters in a short-form play provides a challenge Kushner addresses by making each an archetypal figure à la Brecht. Each announces his or her own defining characteristics, distinguishing professional struggles, and personal yearnings as they all argue over the illicit burial. Curiously it is the deceased Ding who emerges most vividly, both as an inspiration and as an object of affection. Some of the playwrights sadly recall Ding's final days battling HIV/AIDS, while Happy, a bored, rich Hollywood writer whose early plays were much admired, articulates the meaning of the play's title when he explains that HIV "reads and writes its genetic alphabets backwards, RNA transcribing DNA transcribing RNA, hence *retro*virus, reverse transcription," comparing it with reading Hebrew "backwards."[4] Happy explains: "HIV, reverse transcribing, dust to dust, writing backwards, Hebrew and the Great and Terrible magic of that backwards alphabet, which runs against the grain, counter to the current of European traditions, heritage, thought: a language of fiery, consuming revelation, of refusal, the proper way, so I was taught, to address oneself to God" (121). The others argue about the tragedies of AIDS, language, and history, while Happy, backing off equating AIDS with Hebrew, considers the nature of writing, revealing Kushner's thoughts on the subject:

> Writing began with the effort to record speech. All writing is an attempt to fix intangibles—thought, speech, what the eye observes—fixed on clay tablets, in stone, on paper. Writers *capture*. We playwrights on the other hand write or rather "wright" to set these free again. Not inscribing, not de-scribing but . . . ex-scribing (?) . . . "W-R-I-G-H-T," that archaism, because it's something earlier we do, cruder, something one does with one's mitts, one's paws. To claw words up . . . ! (124)

Happy drops to his knees to dig with his hands, to "startle words back into the air again, to . . . Evanesce. It is . . . Unwriting, to do it is to die, yes, but. A lively form of doom," concluding that "it's not about *equation*. It's about the transmutation of horror into meaning" (124).

In 1996 Kushner contributed a one-act play, *Terminating, or Lass Meine Schmerzen Nicht Verloren Sein, or Ambivalence,* inspired by William Shakespeare's Sonnet Seventy-five, to a bill of one-acts written by several contemporary American playwrights, including Eric Bogosian, John Guare, Marsha Norman, Ntozake Shange, Wendy Wasserstein, and William Finn. Titled *Love's Fire,* the bill toured the United States during 1997, culminating in a month-long run at New York's Public Theater in 1998.

Set in a psychiatrist's office, *Terminating* focuses on Hendryk, a wildly disturbed chatterbox intellectual convinced he is in love with his lesbian shrink, Esther. She insists his feelings are transference, to which he replies that all love is transference. Hendryk talks incessantly in a torrent of literary references (in an obvious joke on himself by Kushner), a stream of hilarious contradictions, and bizarre juxtapositions underscoring Kushner's central exploration of the power and failure of language. As the play proceeds, Esther announces that she is terminating Hendryk's therapy, proclaiming him a "godforsaken mess."[5] His response is to beg her to sleep with him. Pointing out that Hendryk is, in fact, gay, he retorts by calling her "a dyke" who wears "*Harley Davidson boots* and you have short hair" (51). Esther is reduced to little more than his foil as Hendryk riffs on the anxieties of late-twentieth-century life, making a bizarre leap to explaining that people get tattooed because of ambivalence—because "tattoos last" (54), a comfort in a rapidly changing world. For Hendryk tattoos are an inscription of existence; no individual can change the world, but skin can be changed, a metaphor suggesting Kushner's anxieties about the difficulty of changing a world needing change.

"Ambivalence," Hendryk states, "expands our options" (55), and shifting back to questions of love, Hendryk announces that he has a beautiful boyfriend with no soul named Billygoat. This relationship bears more than a passing resemblance to the realistically treated, fully dimensioned relationship of Louis and Prior in *Angels in America,* while Esther, as a character, exhibits attributes found in Zillah of *A Bright Room Called Day* and Bonfila of *Slavs!,* similarly strong, troubled women over-whelmed by the demands of their work and consciences. When *Terminating* shifts focus to Esther, she explains that as a lesbian, feminist, and progressive she is distraught to acknowledge that she, too, is ambivalent. What keeps her alive is a "complete lack of hope" (61), for if she were to actually feel hope it would be possible to commit suicide. Esther tries to end the session, par-ticularly after Billygoat and her own lover, Dympha, appear. Dympha laments that "our inability to love one another is humankind's greatest tragedy" (64), but the serious underpin-nings of *Terminating* are submerged in flights of linguistic fancy and in Hendryk's farcical rantings. Critics were approving of *Love's Fire,* with particular praise for *Terminating.*

One additional Kushner one-act written in the late 1990s is a brief, amusing trifle, *And the Torso Even More So,* a "T-shirt" play, written for the 1999 Humana Festival. Kushner comically reveals that even insignificant T-shirts are held together by con-tradictory universal forces. The Woof, his name for the horizon-tal threads, and the Warp (vertical threads) are at odds. The Warp is depressed—his "tight wound soul descends; You'll never understand: I'm *deep, bereft*"—while the Woof is weary of "shuttling through this weave" and longs to unravel his "sleeve of care."[6] Even in a minor riff like this, Kushner's lyricism and existential longings surface.

Kushner completed some screenplays in this period, includ-ing the previously discussed *Grim(m)* and *East Coast Ode to Howard Jarvis,* which gets its title from the elderly Californ-ian who led a grassroots tax revolt in 1978 aimed at curbing burgeoning property taxes. Jarvis became a populist icon and inspired similar tax revolts in other states. *East Coast Ode to Howard Jarvis* was completed for Showtime television in 1996 but never produced. Economically written, the teleplay calls for sixteen men (roles meant to be doubled by eight actors) and seven women (doubled by five actors) in a variety of suggested rather than realistic locations; Kushner hints that a blank photographer's screen might be best for the work's "talking head" characters.

A mock documentary style depicting a mini tax revolt inspired by a scheme created by a midwestern white supremacist, *East Coast Ode to Howard Jarvis* is rife with familiar social types generically identified as Detective, Housing Police, Environmental Protection Officer, and so on, all involved in the revolt and reflecting viewpoints on both sides. A Corrections Officer on Rikers Island who says, "I guess I have always felt I pay too much taxes,"[7] learns from Skinhead Inmate of a scheme devised by the Dutchman, mastermind of the North American White Men's Freedom and Liberty Council, a white supremacist militia group in Indiana. Skinhead Inmate whets the appetite of Corrections Officer for a means of avoiding taxes. A Housing Detective compels his disaffected daughter to use the Internet to contact Dutchman, learning in the process that the organization might be a terrorist front. Only concerned with skirting his taxes, he reaches Dutchman, who refers to the federal government as "the Zionist Occupation Government HQ'd in DC" (4) and who responds with the suggestion that on a W-4 form the number ninety-eight should be placed in the space provided for exemptions, pointing out that no legal limit is set on the number of exemptions a citizen might claim. Dutchman also offers to share literature on the National Rifle Association.

Housing Detective files the W-4 as instructed, and others get wind of the plan and adapt it for themselves. Housing Detective's claim is sent back stamped "ITEMIZE," and he is advised by Dutchman to attach a letter to the W-4, written in legalese, denying citizenship and stating that as an alien he is not subject to taxation. When the letter reaches a Woman in the Payroll Department, an African American, she responds, "Alien to the United States. Baby, I hear what you're saying" (7). In her fifties and living in a tiny apartment, she expresses universal feelings of discontent: "I got no money, I hate my job, I hate this city, I hate my cat, my husband hates his job, this city, the cat, we hate the disappointments, the delays in construction, the bigots, the bozos, the Democrats *and* the Republicans, Newt Gingrich, Bill Clinton, *his* cat, Rudy Giuliani, my insurance company and my boss, the guy playing with himself on the subway at 9AM, the kid with the radio playing at 6AM and I hate the piss smell in the hallway that I have to inhale. Every day" (7). She enters zero in Housing Detective's paycheck withholding and sends it on through the system, absolving herself by saying "let *them* sort it out it is *not* my problem" (8). As the scheme unravels, Housing Detective tries to elicit help from Dutchman, who has "been busted in Cincinnati for crossing state lines with a suitcase full of Uzis, and some bullets, and also he wrote some letter to a US Marshal saying he was gonna whack him or something" (14). The next image reveals Dutchman in a jail cell singing "The Impossible Dream," while a United States Attorney reveals that as many as a thousand New York City employees evaded taxes through Dutchman's scheme. A precociously bright young woman reflects on the American social contract, which she describes:

Um, part of the deal is, like, the people agree to surrender their power to the state. Some of their power. But it's like, *how much?* And it's like, say you the state and I'm the people, did I "lend" you my power and can I fire you if I don't like what you are doing with my power, did I somehow give up my power at birth and now I just got to hope for the best from you, and um, oh yeah, like, is this a contract between authority and each individual or is it, like, a collective expression of a general will towards civilization? (16)

A Woman in the Payroll Department worries about what happens to those who evaded their taxes and expresses a belief that "things coming unglued, that's how it seems to me. Don't it seem like that to you? Everything's just coming apart at the seams. And nobody understands" (17). As with Kushner's plays, the collisions between politics and human nature are central to *East Coast Ode to Howard Jarvis,* a work Kushner frequently read at colleges and universities during the late 1990s.

After several false starts, *Angels in America* finally made it to the screen when the HBO network signed Mike Nichols to direct it as a six-hour miniseries (to be shown in one-hour installments) featuring a stellar cast including Al Pacino, Meryl Streep, Emma Thompson, Justin Kirk, Patrick Wilson, Mary Louise Parker, Jeffrey Wright, and Ben Shenkman, with supporting contributions from James Cromwell, Michael Gambon, and Simon Callow. Kushner and his friend Maurice Sendak appeared in cameo roles as rabbis (Kushner also appeared in a cameo in the 2005 film *The Great New Wonderful*). Critics, even those finding the film too faithful to the plays, were filled with praise, although some questioned Nichols's choice of giving "the characters precedence over the play's polemics."[8] The film is more realistically presented than the play, making selective use of the work's phantasmagoric elements for such significant scenes as a Jean Cocteau–inspired fever dream for Prior and Harper, Harper's encounter with the Mormon Mother in the diorama, and Prior's visitation from the Angel at the end of *Millennium Approaches* and later meeting with the heavenly council of angels in *Perestroika*. The old Bolshevik from *Perestroika* is eliminated, as are selected speeches. The *Angels in America* miniseries was showered with awards, winning an Emmy and a Golden Globe as best TV film, as well as awards for Kushner's screenplay and Nichols's directing. Pacino and Streep won particular acknowledgment, and many critics regarded the acting highlight to be the encounters between Pacino's Roy Cohn and Streep's Ethel Rosenberg (Streep also won praise for her vaunted versatility by playing Hannah Pitt, Rabbi Chemelwitz, and an angel on the heavenly council). *Angels in America* was released on video, and HBO developed a continuing relationship with Kushner, providing financial backing for the Broadway production of *Caroline, or Change*.

Following the *Angels in America* film, Kushner worked on a screenplay about Eugene O'Neill and appeared in a highly praised 2006 PBS documentary about O'Neill. He made occasional television appearances, beginning with a PBS documentary on the New York production of *Angels, In the Wings: Angels in America on Broadway* (1993) and including several appearances on Charlie Rose's PBS talk show beginning in 1994 and as a "talking head" for PBS documentaries about New York City (1999) and Emma Goldman (2004). Similarly he spoke about aspects of his work in the documentaries *Changing Stages* (2000), *Stagestruck: Gay Theatre in the 20th Century* (2000), *The Troupe* (2004), and the symbolic import of angels in *In Search of Angels* (1994). In 2006 Academy Award–winning filmmaker Freida Mock released a film about Kushner, *Wrestling with Angels: Playwright Tony Kushner.* Mock had shadowed Kushner from the time of the 2001 New York Theatre Workshop production of *Homebody/Kabul* through the Broadway opening of *Caroline, or Change* and had documented Kushner's involvement in John Kerry's campaign for the presidency on 2004. Kushner's personal involvement in the national debate over the issue of gay marriage, which most significantly concerned his 2003 marriage to longtime boyfriend Mark Harris, is also central to Mock's film. The much-praised documentary, which includes scenes from Kushner plays and interviews with family and coworkers, was shown in selected cities in late 2006 and on PBS television stations in 2007.

In 2007 Kushner was at work on a screenplay based on Doris Kearns Goodwin's *Team of Rivals,* an account of Abraham Lincoln's leadership during the Civil War, which was expected to star Liam Neeson and Sally Field under the direction of Steven Spielberg. This project, tentatively titled *Lincoln,* resulted from a controversial collaboration between Kushner and Spielberg on *Munich,* a 2005 film directed by Spielberg from a script by Kushner and Eric Roth. Kushner's involvement with *Munich* came well into its production process; based on George Jonas's 1998 book *Vengeance, Munich,* in the form of Roth's initial screenplay, languished until Spielberg convinced Kushner to try writing a few scenes that ultimately turned into a revised screenplay. Spielberg and Kushner continued to revise for a year before the film went before the cameras. As Richard Schickel writes, Kushner "located a dry, allusive, sometimes bleakly comic language"[9] for the characters at the center of a film that is part thriller, part excoriating moral debate. In Kushner's conception, the Munich Olympic murders, seen live on television from their beginning to their bloody end, become a seminal event in contemporary terrorism. Thrust into the lives of international television viewers, the tragic events at Munich are shaped into a complex debate over the moral costs of political violence and revenge.

Kushner frames this event as the first in decades-long terrorist and counterterrorist atrocities stretching from Munich to 9/11 (the final scene shows the World Trade Center in an eerie reminder of the cost of terrorism and revenge) and beyond. Once the inciting act is established, the screenplay focuses on its aftermath as the Israeli government, led by Golda Meir, initiates a covert war of revenge against the planners of the murders. Kushner's Meir states a moral equivocation setting the film's dilemma in motion when she insists, "Every civilization finds it necessary to negotiate compromises with its own values."[10] This statement guides the actions of the state of Israel and is seen through the personal experiences of a few individuals caught up in its circumstances, in this case members of a Mossad hit squad assigned the task of eliminating the perpetrators of the Munich killings. The most anguished figure in the film, Avner Kauffman, the squad's leader, is a decent man grappling with a sense of duty to his people and his own doubt (and guilt) about what he is asked to do and does. Avner leads a double life, one as a husband with a wife and child and another as a professional killer. His fight against Black September and its organizers seems less taxing than his profound struggle to preserve his soul. Joe Klein writes that *Munich* is "about feelings, not facts. It's about the emotional impossibility of a war in which most battles are, of necessity, outside the traditional rules of warfare but also beyond the limits of civilized behavior."[11] Avner becomes an everyman through whom these feelings are examined. Does Avner, a man described as having a butcher's hands but a gentle soul, believe his actions are a means of protecting his wife and infant child, comparatively safe in New York? He treats coworkers as family, plotting their next hit over home-cooked dinners he prepares. His superiors demand obedience, and Avner accepts, believing the cause just. It is only as the mission is carried out, and the body count multiplies, that Avner questions the tactics and probes the moral questions. A war against terrorists is, by its very nature, fought with their rules, which compromise boundaries of morality so-called civilized countries and individuals profess. Avner says, "Eventually, I suppose, you forget you were once someone who really hated doing it,"[12] and Kushner makes sure his audience knows that although Avner will do indecent things and believe he has lost himself, he is not convinced by his own argument—he struggles to hold onto a sense of decency.

When the squad plants a bomb in the home of a Munich planner, the man's little girl unexpectedly returns, raising the danger that an innocent could be killed. Halting the bombing until the child leaves is not a sentimentalizing gesture intended to depict Avner and his colleagues as selfless assassins (although they may well be seen that way); instead their actions and attitudes present the conflict they face: are they cold-blooded killers (soldiers, as Avner describes them) or not? The impossibility of negotiating boundaries between acceptable and unacceptable revenge is presented, as is the inability of the assassins, some of whom have families, to abandon their senses of morality, even though their job requires what in any other circumstance would be deemed atrocities. As such, connections with Kushner's adaptation of *Mother Courage* are obvious.

Kushner and, for his part, Spielberg focus on the fundamental humanity of each individual, terrorist or victim. All have lives, families, and personal problems, and regardless of which side of the eternal Middle Eastern conflicts they find themselves on, each is seen as possessing common humanity. The film's final scene, in which Avner makes love to his wife, increasing in intensity as images of the killings of the athletes and what he has done in the name of Israel flash before him, caused consternation with critics who wondered what this was meant to show. One possibility is that Avner's agonies cannot be assuaged (or forgotten) even in his most intimate moments, while it may also suggest that he and his wife are creating new life to replace those lost. The scene also raises disturbing images of the ways in which violence and sexuality are linked, as other positive and negative human impulses are linked throughout the film. In this Kushner makes use of a device employed in many of his plays, including one of his earliest, a children's theater play, *Yes Yes No No: The Solace-of-Solstice, Apogee/Perigee, Bestial/Celestial Holiday Show* (1985), in which he posits that the universe is powered by friction, by the rubbed-raw pressure of its contradictions. For Avner contradictions emerge as a dense forest of moral ambiguity in which even (or especially) those who see themselves as righteous may experience the painful friction of contradictions that never find resolution, either politically or personally. Can Avner live with what he has done, and can Israel, as a moral nation, survive an act of revenge, even if it is deemed justified? Is reprisal a solution, or does it continue conflict to a point no one wishes to imagine, a point of no return?

Left with the question of the destructiveness of vengeance, whether or not it is in the name of justice, Kushner poses the central question of the new millennium. A way to end the continuing quagmire of violence that engulfs the Middle East and has often and lately drawn in the United States and its allies (as well as its enemies), is, the film suggests, to find a way to end revenge.

The continual spiral of death and destruction interests Kushner less than the question of what violence does to human beings. At the same time, providing a depiction of the reinvention of war as the violent maneuverings of shadowy terrorists, counterterrorists, hit squads, and roadside bombings allows Kushner to wonder how to combat such chaos while he also weighs the ethical questions of participating in it, whether as a society or an individual, justified or not. After private screenings for the families of the Israeli athletes killed at Munich and as *Munich* made its way into theaters, Kushner considered his task in scripting the film: "It's not an essay; it's art. But I think I can safely say the conflict between national security and ethics raised deep questions in terms of working on the film. I was surprised to discover how much the story had to do with nationality vs. family, and questions about home and being in conflict with somebody else over a territory that seems home to both people."[13]

Some critics applauded *Munich* as a "political film,"[14] while others criticized it on the same grounds, lamenting its "lumpy theatrical harangues."[15] Stuart Klawans, writing in the *Nation*, praised *Munich* for having "the internal coherence of a work of art. Its politics are inseparable from its narrative themes, it's characterizations, even its performances,"[16] while *New Yorker* critic Anthony Lane condemned it as "a fidgety, international affair" rife with "cultural clichés [. . .] starting in terror, and ending up on the very brink of kitsch."[17] As controversy mounted, various Jewish and Palestinian organizations entered the fray with editorials debating the issues. Spielberg stated his goals in general terms, while Kushner responded to accusations that he and Spielberg were "apologists for the Palestinians, apologists for Israel, defamers of Palestinians *and* of Israel, softheaded Hollywood liberals, dupes of the radical left, dupes of the radical right, even of being anti-Semitic or self-loathing, for showing Jews talking about receipts and handling money. We're morally confused, overly complicated, simplistic. We're cowards who refused to take sides. We took a side but, oops! the wrong side."[18]

Kushner provides a counter to questions about the veracity of Jonas's book and the reasons he chose to show Mossad agents doubting their mission to kill terrorists. Underscoring the film's assertion that violence inherently has a destructive impact on the person (or nation) committing it, Kushner states, "I've never killed anyone, but my instincts as a person and a playwright—and the best books I've read about soldiers or cops or people whose jobs bring them into violent physical conflict—suggest that people in general don't kill without feeling torn up about it. Violence exacts a psychic toll, unless you're a sociopath, and who wants to watch a movie about a sociopath?"[19] Finally, offering a defense of his views, Kushner acknowledges that he has "been critical of Israel's occupation of the West Bank and Gaza" and the guiding principles behind it:

> I'm an American and a proudly Diasporan Jew. I believe that the best hope for any oppressed minority is found in the Constitution's promise of equal protection under the law, in secular pluralist democracy. I believe that governments—and our souls—are nourished by honesty, open-mindedness and public debate, even of scary ideas and uncomfortable truths. But my criticism of Israel has always been accompanied by declarations of unconditional support of Israel's right to exist, and I believe that the global community has a responsibility to defend that right.[20]

Munich was among the honored films of 2005, receiving Academy Award and Golden Globe nominations as best film and nominations for the Kushner-Roth screenplay.

Among Kushner's work, *Munich* is an overt example of the political nature of his drama, which was central to him from the beginning and garnered significant media attention in the wake of *Angels in America.* Kushner's activism is also expressed outside his dramatic writings, in speeches, essays, periodical columns, and demonstrations. In 1995 he published *Thinking about the Longstanding Problems of Virtue and Happiness,* a collection of writings including speeches and other writings originally published in the *Advocate,* the *Nation,* the *New York Times,* and the *Los Angeles Times.* All offer insight into Kushner's activist agenda, while some query the nature of art and theater. In his public persona, Kushner frequently enters debates on various arts-related controversies, from censorious reactions to *Angels in America* at the Charlotte Repertory Theatre and several colleges, including Catholic University, Kilgore College, and Wabash College, to a major front-page flap over Terrence McNally's *Corpus Christi* at the Manhattan Theatre Club in 1999. Kushner's other essays range across arts-related and political issues, including reflections on Wim Wenders's film *Wings of Desire,* ideas of a Utopian theater, Frank Sinatra's singing, the elimination of undergraduate theater majors, the literature of AIDS (he participated in a 1997 Key West Literary Seminar on the subject, sharing the stage with Larry Kramer), disappointment in Bill Clinton's presidency, Hollywood, Suzan-Lori Parks's play *Venus,* controversy arising from the Nobel Prize presented to leftist playwright-actor Dario Fo, the legacies of Allen Ginsberg and Charles Ludlam, dating in the age of Ken Starr (the Whitewater special prosecutor), the National Endowment of the Arts, and the hate-crime murder of gay University of Wyoming student Matthew Shepard.

Kushner often speaks of the guiding principle marking his work, a "pessimism of the intellect, optimism of the will,"[21] which aims to merge a clear-eyed view of realities with hopefulness about change. His work as a writer and his life as a politically engaged social activist require, in Kushner's view, a belief in progressive change even in the face of personal or societal circumstances mediating against hope. For Kushner finding hope through an exploration of the past, an engaged spirit in the present, and an openness to the unknowable future provides not only inspiration for his work but a strategy for survival.

Appendix

Selected Production History

This listing includes plays and screenplays. The earliest major productions are listed for the plays.

The Age of Assassins
    1982, Newfoundland Theatre, New York, N.Y.

And the Torso Even More So
    February 1999, Humana Festival of New American Plays, Actors Theatre of Louisville, Louisville, Ky.

Angels in America: A Gay Fantasia on National Themes, Part One: Millennium Approaches
    May 1990, Center Theatre Group / Mark Taper Forum, Los Angeles, Calif. (workshop)

    May 1991, Eureka Theater Company, San Francisco, Calif.

    23 January 1992, Royal National Theatre of Great Britain, London, England

    8 November 1992, Mark Taper Forum, Los Angeles, Calif.

    4 May 1993, Walter Kerr Theatre, New York, N.Y.

Angels in America: A Gay Fantasia on National Themes, Part Two: Perestroika
    May 1991, Eureka Theater Company, San Francisco, Calif.

    May 1992, Mark Taper Forum, Los Angeles, Calif. (workshop)

    8 November 1992, Mark Taper Forum, Los Angeles, Calif.

    April 1993, New York University / Tisch School of the Arts, New York, N.Y.

    20 November 1993, Royal National Theatre of Great Britain, London, England

    23 November 1993, Walter Kerr Theatre, New York, N.Y.

A Bright Room Called Day

    22 April 1985, Heat & Light Company, Inc., Theatre 22, New York, N.Y. (workshop)

    October 1987, Eureka Theater Company, San Francisco, Calif.

    July 1988, Bush Theatre, London, England

    7 January 1991, New York Public Theater, New York, N.Y.

Caroline, or Change

    May 1999, New York Public Theater's New Work Now! (workshop), New York, N.Y.

    November 2003, New York Public Theater, New York, N.Y.

    2 May 2004, Eugene O'Neill Theater, New York, N.Y.

    19 October 2006, Lyttleton Theatre, National Theatre of Great Britain, London, England

A Dybbuk, or Between Two Worlds (adapted from the Yiddish theatre play by S. Ansky)

    February 1995, Hartford Stage Company, New Haven, Conn.

    January 1996, Denver Center Theatre, Denver, Colo.

    November 1997, New York Public Theater, New York, N.Y.

East Coast Ode to Howard Jarvis

    1996, unproduced

La Fin de la Baleine: An Opera for the Apocalypse

    1983, Ohio Theatre, New York, N.Y.

G. David Schine in Hell

    1996, unproduced

The Good Person of Setzuan (adapted from the play by Bertolt Brecht)

    July 1994, La Jolla Playhouse, La Jolla, Calif.

    June 1999, Wings Theatre, New York, N.Y.

Grim(m) (inspired by the Brothers Grimm's story "The Two Journeymen")

    1995, unproduced

The Heavenly Theatre

    1986, New York University's Tisch School of the Arts, New York, N.Y.

Henry Box Brown, or The Mirror of Slavery

    1997, work in progress

Historiomax

    1985, unproduced

Home Body

    July 1999, Chelsea Theatre Centre, London, England

Homebody/Kabul

    19 December 2001, New York Theatre Workshop, New York, N.Y.

    15 March 2002, Trinity Repertory Company, Providence, R.I.

    19 April 2002, Berkeley Repertory Theatre, Berkeley, Calif.

    10 May 2002, Young Vic, London, England

    20 July 2003, Steppenwolf Theatre, Chicago, Ill.

    17 September 2003, Intiman Theatre, Seattle, Wash.

    2 October 2003, Mark Taper Forum, Los Angeles, Calif.

    May 2004, Brooklyn Academy of Music, Brooklyn, N.Y.

Hydriotaphia, or The Death of Dr. Browne

    1987, Home for Contemporary Theatre and Art, New York, N.Y.

    April 1997, New York University / Tisch School of the Arts, New York, N.Y.

    March 1998, Alley Theatre, Houston, Tex.

    September 1998, Berkeley Repertory Theatre, Berkeley, Calif.

The Illusion (freely adapted from the play by Pierre Corneille)

    19 October 1988, New York Theatre Workshop, New York, N.Y.

    29 December 1989, Hartford Stage Company, Hartford, Conn.

    30 March 1990, Los Angeles Theatre Center, Los Angeles, Calif.

June 1991, Berkeley Repertory Theatre, Berkeley, Calif.

October 1991, Los Angeles Theatre Center, Los Angeles, Calif.

19 January 1994, Classic Stage Company, New York, N.Y.

In Great Eliza's Golden Time

1986, Imaginary Theatre Company, Repertory Theatre of St. Louis, St. Louis, Mo.

In That Day; Lives of the Prophets

1989, New York University / Tisch School of the Arts, New York, N.Y.

"It's an Undoing World," or Why Should It Be Easy When It Can Be Hard?

1995, Los Angeles Modern Dance and Ballet Company, Los Angeles, Calif.

Last Gasp at the Cataract

1984, The Yard, Martha's Vineyard, Mass.

Mother Courage and Her Children

8 August 2006, Delacorte Theater, New York, N.Y.

Munich (film)

Released 6 January 2006

Notes on Akiba

13 April 1995, New York Jewish Museum, New York, N.Y.

The Protozoa Review

1985

Reverse Transcription: Six Playwrights Bury a Seventh; A Ten-Minute Play That's Nearly Twenty Minutes Long

March 1996, Humana Festival of New American Plays, Actors Theatre of Louisville, Louisville, Ky.

Slavs! Thinking about the Longstanding Problems of Virtue and Happiness

8 March 1994, Humana Festival of New American Plays, Actors Theatre of Louisville, Louisville, Ky.

6 June 1994, Lesbian Avengers Civil Rights Organizing Project, Walter Kerr Theatre, New York, N.Y.

June 1994, Steppenwolf Theatre Company, Chicago, Ill.

12 December 1994, New York Theatre Workshop, New York

St. Cecilia, or The Power of Music (adapted from the story by Heinrich von Kleist)

1997, unproduced

Stella: A Play for Lovers (adapted from the play by Johann Wolfgang von Goethe)

1987, New York Theatre Workshop, New York, N.Y.

Terminating, or Lass Meine Schmerzen Nicht Verloren Sein, or Ambivalence (inspired by William Shakespeare's Sonnet Seventy-five)

7 January 1998, The Guthrie Theater Lab, Minneapolis, Minn.

July 1998, New York Public Theater, New York, N.Y.

The Umbrella Oracle

1984, The Yard, Martha's Vineyard, Mass.

Widows (coadapted with Ariel Dorfman from the novel by Dorfman)

24 July 1991, Mark Taper Forum, Los Angeles, Calif.

Yes Yes No No: The Solace-of-Solstice, Apogee/Perigee, Bestial/Celestial Holiday Show

1986, Imaginary Theatre Company, Repertory Theatre of St. Louis, St. Louis, Mo.

Notes

Chapter 1—Understanding Tony Kushner

1. Octavio Roca, "Kushner's Next Stage; Award-Winning Playwright's *Hydriotaphia* Opens Season at Berkeley Rep," *San Francisco Chronicle,* 6 September 1998, 32.

2. Ernst Fischer, *The Necessity of Art: A Marxist Approach,* trans. Anna Bostock (New York: Penguin Books, 1963), 14.

3. Robert H. Vorlicky, ed., *Tony Kushner in Conversation* (Ann Arbor: University of Michigan Press, 1998), 63.

4. Alex Abramovich, "Hurricane Kushner Hits the Heartland," *New York Times,* 30 November 2003, sec. 2, 5.

5. Walter Benjamin, *Illuminations: Essays and Reflections,* ed. Hannah Arendt, trans. Harry Zohn (New York: Schocken Books, 1968), 256–57.

6. David Savran, "Tony Kushner," in *Speaking on Stage: Interviews with Contemporary American Playwrights,* ed. Philip C. Kolin and Colby H. Kullman (Tuscaloosa: University of Alabama Press, 1996), 300.

7. Ibid.

8. Frederic Tuten, "Writing the Playwright: Tony Kushner in Conversation with Frederic Tuten," *Guernica Magazine,* June 2005, n.p.

9. Ibid.

10. Wendell Brock, "Events Thrust Kushner's 'Kabul' into the Spotlight," *Atlanta Journal-Constitution,* 30 March 2003, M6.

11. Ibid.

12. John Lahr, "Earth Angels," *New Yorker,* 13 December 1993, 133.

13. Tony Kushner, *Angels in America, Part One: Millennium Approaches* (New York: Theatre Communications Group, 1993), 117.

14. Jane Edwardes, "Kabul's Eye," *Time Out,* 30 June–7 July 1999, n.p.

15. Vorlicky, *Tony Kushner in Conversation,* 278.

16. Ibid., 218.

17. Patrick Pacheco, "AIDS, Angels, Activism, and Sex in the Nineties," *Body Positive,* September 1993, 17.

18. Tony Kushner, "Notes about Political Theater," *Kenyon Review* 19 (Summer–Fall 1997): 22.

19. James Poniewozik, "What's Entertainment Now?" *Time,* 1 October 2001, 112.

Chapter 2—Early Plays

1. Travis Mader, "Tony Kushner and Dr. Browne," *Alley Theatre Newsletter,* Spring 1998, 1.

2. Tony Kushner, *Death and Taxes: "Hydriotaphia" and Other Plays* (New York: Theatre Communications Group, 2000), 143. Subsequent references to *Hydriotaphia, or The Death of Dr. Browne* from this edition are noted parenthetically.

3. Everett Evans, "Last Laughs; 17th-Century Essay Inspires 'Epic Farce' on Life and Death," *Houston Chronicle,* 29 March 1998, 11.

4. Mader, "Tony Kushner and Dr. Browne," 1.

5. Ibid.

6. Ibid.

7. Ibid.

8. Ibid.

9. Octavio Roca, "Kushner's Next Stage; Award-Winning Playwright's *Hydriotaphia* Opens Season at Berkeley Rep," *San Francisco Chronicle,* 6 September 1998, 32.

10. Evans, "Last Laughs," 10.

11. Ibid.

12. Mader, "Tony Kushner and Dr. Browne," 1.

13. Ibid., 1, 5.

14. Evans, "Last Laughs," 11.

15. Roca, "Kushner's Next Stage," 32.

16. Remy., "*A Bright Room Called Day*," *Variety*, 14 January 1991, 118.

17. Tony Kushner, *A Bright Room Called Day* (New York: Theatre Communications Group, 1994), 183. Subsequent references to this edition are noted parenthetically.

18. David Richards, "Tale of One City Set in Two Times—Both Fearful," *New York Times*, 13 January 1991, 5.

19. Linda Winer, "Evils of Humanity Crowd *Bright Room*," *New York Newsday*, 8 January 1991, 44.

20. Irene Oppenheim, "Shedding More Light on *Bright Room*," *American Theatre*, September 2000, 75.

21. Violet Woodward, "*Bright* Offers Political Comments," *Yale Daily News*, 12 November 2004, n.p.

22. Roy Sander, review of *A Bright Room Called Day*, *Back Stage*, 18 January 1991, 48.

Chapter 3—*Angels in America*

1. Raymond Williams, *Resources of Hope: Culture, Democracy, Socialism*, ed. Robin Gale (London and New York: Verso, 1989), 283.

2. Tony Kushner, *Angels in America, Part Two: Perestroika* (New York: Theatre Communications Group, 1994), 148. Subsequent references to this play are noted parenthetically.

3. Tony Kushner, *Angels in America, Part One: Millennium Approaches* (New York: Theatre Communications Group, 1993). Subsequent references to this play are noted parenthetically.

4. Barry Joseph, "Tony Kushner, Native Son," *In These Times*, 4 March 2002, 29.

5. Anne Fleche, *Mimetic Disillusion: Eugene O'Neill, Tennessee Williams, and U.S. Dramatic Realism* (Tuscaloosa: University of Alabama Press, 1997), 110.

6. Walter Benjamin, *Illuminations: Essays and Reflections*, ed. Hannah Arendt, trans. Harry Zohn (New York: Schocken Books, 1968), 257–58.

7. Anna Quindlen, "Happy and Gay," *New York Times,* 16 April 1994, A21.

8. Tony Kushner, *Death and Taxes: "Hydriotaphia" and Other Plays* (New York: Theatre Communications Group, 2000), 232. Subsequent references to *G. David Schine in Hell,* published in this volume, are noted parenthetically.

9. Tony Kushner, *Thinking about the Longstanding Problems of Virtue and Happiness: Essays, a Play, Two Poems, and a Prayer* (New York: Theatre Communications Group, 1995), 108. Subsequent references to *Slavs! Thinking about the Longstanding Problems of Virtue and Happiness,* published in this volume, are noted parenthetically.

10. Vincent Canby, "In Slavs! Kushner Creates Tragic Burlesque," *New York Times,* 18 December 1994, sec. 2, 5.

11. John Lahr, "Hail, Slovonia," *New Yorker,* 9 January 1995, 85.

Chapter 4—*Homebody/Kabul*

1. Michael Phillips, "After the Attack: Media/Culture; Tony Kushner: 'It's No Time for Silence,'" *Los Angeles Times,* 22 September 2001, sec. 6, 1.

2. John Podhoertz, "Tony Kushner's Afghanistan; Even an America-Hater Has His Limits," *Weekly Standard,* 11 February 2002, 21.

3. Tony Kushner and Naomi Wallace, "Grist for a Writer's Mill," *American Theatre,* October 2001, 37.

4. Tony Kushner, *Homebody/Kabul,* rev. ed. (New York: Theatre Communications Group, 2004), 28. A prior version of *Homebody/Kabul* was published by TCG in 2002. Subsequent references to *Homebody/Kabul* are from the 2004 revised edition and are noted parenthetically.

5. Jess Cagle and Jeanne McDowell, "The Culture," *Time,* 1 October 2001, 112.

6. "Reflections on an America Transformed," *New York Times,* 8 September 2002, 15.

7. Phillips, "After the Attack," 1.

8. Ibid.

9. Tony Kushner, *Only We Who Guard the Mystery Shall Be Unhappy, Nation,* 24 March 2003, 15.

10. Blake Green, "His Very Own Scoop," *Los Angeles Times,* 16 December 2001, sec. 6, 7.

11. Framji Minwalla, "Tony Kushner's *Homebody/Kabul:* Staging History in a Post-Colonial World," *Theater* 33 (Winter 2003): 42.

12. Phillips, "After the Attack," 1.

13. Ibid.

14. Barry Joseph, "Tony Kushner, Native Son," *In These Times,* 4 March 2002, 29.

15. Tony Kushner, e-mail to author, 25 March 2002.

16. Marc Peyser, "Tales from Behind Enemy Lines," *Newsweek,* 17 December 2001, 68.

17. Minwalla, "Tony Kushner's *Homebody/Kabul,*" 38.

18. James Reston Jr., "A Prophet in His Time," *American Theatre,* March 2002, 53.

19. Desmond Ryan, "Bold Drama, Predating 9/11, Reflects on Afghanistan," *Philadelphia Inquirer,* 3 February 2002, H6.

20. Amy Barrett, "The Way We Live Now: Questions for Tony Kushner," *New York Times,* 7 October 2001, sec. 6, 23.

21. John Heilpern, "Zounds! Kushner's *Homebody/Kabul* Is Our Best Play in Last 10 Years," *New York Observer,* 5 January 2002, 1.

Chapter 5—*Caroline, or Change*

1. Tony Kushner, *Caroline, or Change* (New York: Theatre Communications Group, 2004). Subsequent references to this edition are noted parenthetically.

2. Jeremy McCarter, "Is Tony Kushner Psychic? The Relevance of His Plays," *New York Magazine,* 19 September 2004, 68.

3. Ibid.

4. "Sweet Caroline: Tony Kushner Gets Lyrical," *New York,* 27 October 2003, 102.

5. Pat Craig, "Kushner's 'Caroline' Hits Some Serious Notes," *Contra Costa Times,* 14 January 2005, D1.

6. John Lahr, "Underwater Blues," *New Yorker,* 8 December 2003, 123.

7. Frank Rich, "'Caroline,' Kennedy and Change," *New York Times,* 7 December 2003, sec. 2, 24.

8. Ibid.

9. Adam Feldman, "Divalution," *Time Out New York,* 3–10 June 2004, 16.

10. Robert Simonson, "Goodnight, Moon: Kushner-Tesori Musical *Caroline, or Change* Begins Previews," *Playbill,* 29 October 2003.

11. Karen D'Souza, "Mixed Reception Doesn't Dim Playwright's Pride in Musical," *Mercury News,* 16 January 2005, 1C.

12. Richard Goldstein, "Angels in a Changed America," *Village Voice,* 26 November–2 December 2003.

13. Simonson, "Goodnight, Moon."

14. Mel Gussow, "Write It, Stage It, Tweak It: Tony Kushner Continues to Tinker with *Homebody/Kabul,*" *New York Times,* 9 September 2002, E5.

15. Robert Simonson, "Kushner Addresses Caroline, Producers, Critics in League Speech," *Playbill,* 27 May 2004, n.p.

16. "Sweet Caroline: Tony Kushner Gets Lyrical," 102.

17. Lahr, "Underwater Blues," 123.

18. Tony Kushner, *Angels in America, Part One: Millennium Approaches* (New York: Theatre Communications Group, 1993), 10.

19. John Simon, "'S Wonderful," *New York,* 8 December 2003, 71.

20. Michael Feingold, "Southern Composure," *Village Voice,* 3–9 December 2002.

Chapter 6—Adaptations

1. Tony Kushner, *The Illusion* (New York: Theatre Communications Group, 1994), 82. Freely adapted from Pierre Corneille. Subsequent references to this edition of *The Illusion* are noted parenthetically.

2. David Richards, "Kushner's Adaptation of a French Classic," *New York Times,* 20 January 1994, C16.

3. Johann Wolfgang von Goethe, *Goethe: The Collected Works,* vol. 7, *Early Verse Drama and Prose Plays,* ed. Cyrus Hamlin and Frank Ryder (Princeton, N.J.: Princeton University Press, 1988), 190.

4. Tony Kushner, "Stella: A Play for Lovers," unpublished first draft dated 11 July 1996, I.2. Freely adapted from Goethe. Subsequent references to this unpublished adaptation of "Stella: A Play for Lovers" are from this draft and noted parenthetically as Kushner numbers acts and pages in the text.

5. Tony Kushner, "St. Cecilia, or The Power of Music," unpublished first draft dated 1 September 1997, I.i.1. Subsequent references to this unpublished adaptation of "St. Cecilia, or The Power of Music" are noted parenthetically as Kushner numbers acts, scenes, and pages in the text.

6. Jordan Mann, "The Good Person of La Jolla," *Theater Week,* 18–24 July 1994, 22.

7. Tony Kushner, "Widows," unpublished undated draft, 96. Adapted from Ariel Dorfman's novel.

8. Ibid., 23.

9. Tony Kushner, "Grim(m)," unpublished second draft dated 11 August 1995, 4. After "The Two Journeymen" by the Brothers Grimm. Subsequent references to this unpublished screenplay for "Grim(m)" are noted parenthetically.

10. Raymond Williams, *Drama: From Ibsen to Brecht* (New York: Oxford University Press, 1969), 290.

11. Mann, "The Good Person of La Jolla," 22.

12. Robert H. Vorlicky, ed., *Tony Kushner in Conversation* (Ann Arbor: University of Michigan Press, 1998), 119.

13. Tony Kushner, "The Good Person of Setzuan," unpublished first draft dated 1995, 180. Adapted from Bertolt Brecht. Subsequent references to this unpublished adaptation of "The Good Person of Setzuan" are noted parenthetically.

14. Vorlicky, *Tony Kushner in Conversation,* 122.

15. Ibid., 111.

16. Mann, "The Good Person of La Jolla," 22.

17. Ibid., 23.

18. Ibid.

19. Vorlicky, *Tony Kushner in Conversation,* 203.

20. Mann, "The Good Person of La Jolla," 22.

21. Ibid.

22. Ibid.

23. Ibid.

24. Vorlicky, *Tony Kushner in Conversation,* 119.

25. Ibid.

26. Jeff Britton, "Modern Twist Sharpens SD's *Good Person,*" *Long Beach Blade,* August 1994.

27. Vorlicky, *Tony Kushner in Conversation,* 123.

28. Ben Brantley, "Mother, Courage, Grief and Song," *New York Times,* 22 August 2006.

29. Eric Grode, "March On, Meryl Streep," *New York Sun,* 22 August 2006.

30. Peter Marks, "When Courage Is Not Enough, Even for Streep," *Washington Post,* 23 August 2006, C1.

31. Joe Dziemianowicz, "In *Courage,* Streep Braves Ill-Fitting Role," *New York Daily News,* 22 August 2006, 37.

32. Grode, "March On, Meryl Streep."

33. Jonathan Kalb, "Still Fearsome, Mother Courage Gets a Makeover," *New York Times,* 6 August 2006, 4.

34. Ibid.

35. Jeremy McCarter, "The Courage of Their Convictions," *New York Magazine,* 25 August 2006.

36. Kalb, "Still Fearsome," 4.

37. Ibid.

38. Ibid.

39. Dziemianowicz, "In *Courage,*" 37.

40. Toby Zinman, "Streep and Brecht, Free and Marvelous," *Philadelphia Inquirer,* 22 August 2006.

41. Grode, "March On, Meryl Streep."

42. Hilton Als, "Wagon Train," *New Yorker,* 4 September 2006, 132.

43. Ibid.

44. Harold Bloom, afterword in *A Dybbuk and Other Tales of the Supernatural,* by Tony Kushner and Joachim Neugroschel, adapted and trans. from S. Ansky (New York: Theatre Communications Group, 1998), 109.

45. Tony Kushner, *"It's an Undoing World," or Why Should It Be Easy When It Can Be Hard?* in *Conjunctions: 25, The New American Theater,* ed. John Guare (Annandale-on-Hudson, N.Y.: Bard College, 1995), 15.

46. Alisa Solomon, *Re-dressing the Canon: Essays on Theatre and Gender* (London and New York: Routledge, 1997), 121–22.

47. Vorlicky, *Tony Kushner in Conversation,* 224.

48. Ibid.

49. Solomon, *Re-dressing the Canon,* 121–22.

50. Tony Kushner and Joachim Neugroschel, *A Dybbuk and Other Tales of the Supernatural,* adaped.and trans. from S. Ansky (New York: Theatre Communications Group, 1998), 86. Subsequent references to this edition of *A Dybbuk and Other Tales of the Supernatural* are noted parenthetically.

51. Vorlicky, *Tony Kushner in Conversation,* 225–26.

Chapter 7—Screenplays and Other Writings

1. Robert H. Vorlicky, ed., *Tony Kushner in Conversation* (Ann Arbor: University of Michigan Press, 1998), 123.

2. Peter Marks, "On Stage, and Off," *New York Times,* 28 June 1996, C2.

3. Christopher Hawthorne, "Coming Out as a Socialist," *Salon,* 18 April 1996, http://www.salon.com/weekly/interview960610.html (accessed ca. 2000).

4. Tony Kushner, *Reverse Transcription: Six Playwrights Bury a Seventh; A Ten-Minute Play That's Nearly Twenty Minutes Long,* in *Humana Festival '96: The Complete Plays,* ed. Michael Bigelow

Dixon and Liz Engelman (Lyme, N.H.: Smith and Kraus, 1996), 121. Subsequent references to *Reverse Transcription* are noted parenthetically.

5. Tony Kushner, *Terminating, or Lass Meine Schmerzen Nicht Verloren Sein, or Ambivalence,* in *Love's Fire: Seven New Plays Inspired by Seven Shakespearean Sonnets,* by Eric Bogosian, William Finn, John Guare, Tony Kushner, Marsha Norman, Ntozake Shange, and Wendy Wasserstein (New York: William Morrow, 1998), 47. Subsequent references to *Terminating* are noted parenthetically.

6. Tony Kushner, *And the Torso Even More So,* in *Humana Festival '99: The Complete Plays,* ed. Michael Bigelow Dixon and Amy Wegener (Lyme, N.H.: Smith and Kraus, 1999), 305.

7. Tony Kushner, "East Coast Ode to Howard Jarvis," unpublished third draft, 8 January 1997, 1. Subsequent references to this unpublished screenplay are noted parenthetically.

8. Alessandra Stanley, "Finally, TV Drama to Argue About," *New York Times,* 30 November 2003, sec. 2, 38.

9. Richard Schickel, "Spielberg Takes on Terror," *Time,* 12 December 2005, 67.

10. Tony Kushner and Eric Roth, "Munich," unpublished screenplay based on the book *Vengeance* by George Jonas, 2005, 21.

11. Joe Klein, "When Hollywood Gets Terrorism Right," *Time,* 9 January 2006, 21.

12. Kushner and Roth, "Munich," 136.

13. Schickel, "Spielberg Takes on Terror," 66–67.

14. Ken Tucker, "Hit Job," *New York,* 26 December 2005–2 January 2006, 111.

15. Anthony Lane, "The Other," *New Yorker,* 26 December 2005–2 January 2006, 149.

16. Stuart Klawans, "A History of Violence," *Nation,* 9–16 January 2006, 32.

17. Lane, "The Other," 150.

18. Tony Kushner, "Defending *Munich* to My Mishpocheh," *Los Angeles Times,* 22 January 2006, M1.

19. Ibid.

20. Ibid.

21. Jane Edwardes, "Kabul's Eye," *Time Out,* 30 June–7 July 1999. n.p.

Bibliography

Published Works by Tony Kushner

Plays

"*And the Torso Even More So.*" In *Humana Festival '99: The Complete Plays,* edited by Michael Bigelow Dixon and Amy Wegener, 303–5. Lyme, N.H.: Smith and Kraus, 1999.

Angels in America, Part One: Millennium Approaches. London: National Theatre / Nick Hern, 1992; New York: Theatre Communications Group, 1993.

Angels in America, Part Two: Perestroika. London: National Theatre / Nick Hern, 1994; New York: Theatre Communications Group, 1994.

Angels in America, Part One: Millennium Approaches / Angels in America, Part Two: Perestroika. New York: Theatre Communications Group, 1995.

Angels in America: A Gay Fantasia on National Themes; Part One: Millennium Approaches; Part Two: Perestroika. New York: Theatre Communications Group, 1994. Paperback two-volume edition of the previously published single-play versions.

Angels in America: A Gay Fantasia on National Themes; Part One: Millennium Approaches; Part Two: Perestroika. New York: Theatre Communications Group, 1995. Hardbound edition in one volume that includes both *Angels in America* plays, with a revised version of *Perestroika* and numerous illustrations of international productions of the play.

A Backstage Pass to Hell. In *New York Times Magazine*, 29 December 1996, sec. 6, 22–23. This short one-act play is also known as *G. David Schine in Hell.*

A Bright Room Called Day. New York: Theatre Communications Group, 1987, 1992, 1994. Also included in *Seven Different Plays,* edited by Mac Wellman. New York: Broadway Play Publishing, 1988.

But the Giraffe, a Curtain Raiser, and Brundibár, a Libretto. Illustrations by Maurice Sendak. New York: Theatre Communications Group, 2007.

Caroline, or Change. New York: Theatre Communications Group, 2004. *Caroline, or Change* was also recorded in its entirety and released on a two-CD set by Hollywood Records as an original Broadway cast recording.

Death and Taxes: "Hydriotaphia" and Other Plays. New York: Theatre Communications Group, 1998.

A Dybbuk and Other Tales of the Supernatural. New York: Theatre Communications Group, 1997. The Klezmatics, who played live, original music for the New York Public Theater production of *A Dybbuk*, released a CD of the music called *Possessed* on the Xenophile Records label in 1997.

Homebody/Kabul. New York: Theatre Communications Group, 2002. Revised edition, 2005.

The Illusion. New York: Theatre Communications Group, 1994. New York: Broadway Play Publishing, 2003. Adapted from Pierre Corneille's play.

"It's an Undoing World," or Why Should It Be Easy When It Can Be Hard? In *Conjunctions: 25, The New American Theater,* edited by John Guare, 14–37. Annandale-on-Hudson, N.Y.: Bard College, 1995.

Notes on Akiba. In *Too Jewish? Challenging Traditional Identities,* edited by Norman L. Kleeblatt, 114–27. New York: The Jewish Museum (under the auspices of the Jewish Theological Seminary of America) and New Brunswick, N.J.: Rutgers University Press, 1996.

Only We Who Guard the Mystery Shall Be Unhappy. Nation, 24 March 2003, 11–15.

Plays by Tony Kushner. New York: Broadway Play Publishing, 1992, 1999.

Reverse Transcription. In *Humana Festival '96: The Complete Plays,* edited by Michael Bigelow Dixon and Liz Engelman, 113–25. Lyme, N.H.: Smith and Kraus, 1996. Also in *Take Ten: New 10-Minute Plays.* New York: Vintage Books, 1997.

Slavs! Thinking about the Longstanding Problems of Virtue and Happiness. New York: Broadway Play Publishing, 1996. Also included in *Humana Festival '94: The Complete Plays,* edited by Marisa Smith. Lyme, N.H.: Smith and Kraus, 1994.

Terminating, or Lass Meine Schmerzen Nicht Verloren Sein, or Ambivalence. In *Love's Fire: Seven New Plays Inspired by Seven Shakespearean Sonnets*, by Eric Bogosian, William Finn, John Guare, Tony Kushner, Marsha Norman, Ntozake Shange, and Wendy Wasserstein. New York: William Morrow, 1998.

"*Viudas (Widows).*" With Ariel Dorfman. In *Teatro 2 (Lector, Viudas),* by Dorfman. Buenos Aires, Argentina: Ediciones de la Flor, 1996.

"*Yes Yes No No: The Solace-of-Solstice, Apogee/Perigee Bestial/ Celestial Holiday Show.*" In *Plays in Process: Three Plays for Young Audiences.* Vol. 7, no. 11. New York: Theatre Communications Group, 1987.

Books by Kushner

The Art of Maurice Sendak: 1980 to the Present. New York: Harry N. Abrams, 2003.

Brundibar. Illustrated by Maurice Sendak. New York: Michael di Capua Books, 2003.

A Meditation from Angels in America: A Folding Screen Book. With Charles Rue Woods. San Francisco: HarperSan Francisco, 1994.

A Prayer. New York: Theatre Communications Group, 1995. Reprinted in *Thinking about the Longstanding Problems of Virtue and Happiness: Essays, a Play, Two Poems, and a Prayer.* New York: Theatre Communications Group, 1995.

Thinking about the Longstanding Problems of Virtue and Happiness: Essays, a Play, Two Poems, and a Prayer. New York: Theatre Communications Group, 1995.

Wrestling with Zion: Progressive Jewish-American Responses to the Israeli-Palestinian Conflict. Edited by Tony Kushner and Alisa Solomon. New York: Grove Press, 2003.

Selected Articles by Kushner

"The Art of the Difficult." *Civilization* 4 (August–September 1997): 62–67. Kushner discusses the nature of politically engaged playwriting.

"Copious, Gigantic, and Sane." *Los Angeles Times,* 25 April 1993, sec. M. Also appears in *The Routledge Reader in Politics and Performance*, edited by Lizbeth Goodman with Jane de Gay, 178–80. London and New York: Routledge, 2000. A rumination on gay activism and drama.

"Defending *Munich* to My Mishpocheh." *Los Angeles Times,* 22 January 2006, M1. After an encounter with his cousin at a family event, Kushner considers the controversy over *Munich*.

"Fighting the Arts Bullies." *Nation,* 29 November 1999, 41–42. Kushner responds to conservative forces attempting to halt a production of Terrence McNally's *Corpus Christi* at the Manhattan Theatre Club.

Foreword to *Body Blows: Six Performances,* by Tim Miller. Madison: University of Wisconsin Press, 2002.

Foreword to *The Design of Dissent,* by Milton Glaser and Mirko Ili. Gloucester, Mass.: Rockport Publishers, 2005.

Foreword to *A Heiner Müller Reader: Plays, Poetry, Prose,* edited by Carl Weber. PAJ Books. Baltimore: Johns Hopkins University Press, 2001.

Foreword to *Staging Gay Lives: An Anthology of Contemporary Gay Theater,* edited by John M. Clum. Boulder, Colo.: Westview Press, 1996.

Foreword to *The Theatre Quotation Book: A Treasury of Insights and Insults,* by Russell Vandenbroucke. New York: Limelight Editions, 2002.

"Fo's Last Laugh—I." *Nation,* 3 November 1997, 4–5. Kushner discusses the significance of the leftist political playwright-actor Dario Fo in the wake of Fo's winning a Nobel Prize for literature.

"Gay Perestroika." *Advocate,* 23 December 1997, 72.

"Gays in the Military: The Pursuit of Social Justice." *Los Angeles Times,* 31 January 1993, M1, 6.

"Holding Our Noses." *Advocate,* 29 October 1996, 53.

"I Am Your Newt." *Advocate,* 24 June 1995, 10.

"I Have a Dream." *Advocate,* 18 October 1994, 8.

Introduction to *Arthur Miller: Collected Plays, 1944–1961,* by Arthur Miller. New York: Library of America, 2006.

Introduction to *The Greek Plays,* by Ellen McLaughlin. New York: Theatre Communications Group, 2004.

Introduction to *The Mystery of Irma Vep and Other Plays,* by Charles Ludlam. New York: Consortium Books, 2000.

Introduction to *The Normal Heart and The Destiny of Me,* by Larry Kramer. New York: Grove Press, 2000.

Introduction to *Peter's Pixie*, by Donn Kushner and Sylvie Daigneault. New York: Tundra Books, 2003.

Introduction to *The Queen's Desire: Opera, Homosexuality, and the Mystery of Desire*, by Wayne Koestenbaum. New York: Da Capo Press, 2001.

Introduction to *Queer and Loathing: Rants and Raves of a Raging AIDS Clone*, by David B. Feinberg. New York: Penguin, 1995.

Introduction to *Seven Guitars,* by August Wilson. New York: Theatre Communications Group, 2007.

Introduction to *Stuck Rubber Baby,* by Howard Cruse. New York: Harper Perennial, 1996.

Introduction to *Tales of the Lost Formicans and Other Plays,* by Constance Congdon. New York: Theatre Communications Group, 1994.

Introduction to *The Waterfront Journals,* edited by David Wojnarowicz and Amy Scholder. New York: Grove/Atlantic, 1996.

"Is It a Fiction That Playwrights Create Alone?" *New York Times,* 21 November 1993, sec. 2, 1, 30–31. Kushner discusses the impact of collaborators and inspirations on a playwright's work.

"Key West Weekend." *Advocate,* 4 March 1997, 64. Kushner describes a writers' conference he attended.

"The Lawyer, the Poet." *Advocate,* 27 May 1997, 104.

"Matthew's Passion." *Nation,* 9 November 1998, 4–6. Kushner writes in anger and in grief over the hate-crime murder of gay college student Matthew Shepard.

"A Modest Proposal." *American Theatre,* January 1998, 20–22, 77–89. Kushner's keynote address to the Association for Theatre in Higher Education, in which, among other things, he suggests the elimination of theater training programs on the undergraduate level.

"Notes about Political Theater." *Kenyon Review* 19 (Summer–Fall 1997): 19–34. Kushner examines the value of political drama and his own work as a political dramatist.

"On Pretentiousness." In *Taking Liberties: Gay Men's Essays on Politics, Culture, and Sex*, edited by Michael Bronski, 207–27. New York: Richard Kasak, 1996.

"Outtakes from *Perestroika.*" *Theater Week,* 17–23 January 1994, 22–25. Bits of dialogue and business cut from *Perestroika,* the second *Angels in America* play.

"A Prayer." In *Gay Men at the Millennium: Sex, Spirit, Community,* edited by Michael Lowenthal, 170–76. New York: Jeremy P. Tarcher / Putnam, 1997. Kushner's AIDS Day prayer, which commemorates those who have died from or are stricken with HIV/AIDS and condemns the governmental and religious forces that he suggests have not done enough to stem the tide of the pandemic.

"Problems of My Own." *Advocate,* 31 March 1998, 88.

"Rants and Raves." *Advocate,* 13 October 1998, 10.

"Reflections on an America Transformed." *New York Times,* 8 September 2002, 15. Along with other public figures, Kushner writes reflections on the year following the attacks on the World Trade Center and the Pentagon on 9/11.

"Remembering Frank." *Advocate,* 23 June 1998, 136. An essay memorializing Frank Sinatra as the most "femme" of American popular singers.

"The Secrets of *Angels* (as Told to William Harris)." *New York Times,* 27 March 1994, H5. Kushner explains aspects of the *Angels in America* plays.

"Sex Is Still Worth It." *Esquire,* October 1993, 158. Kushner writes of the continuing joys of sexuality despite the fears generated by AIDS.

"A Socialism of the Skin (Liberation, Honey!)." *Nation,* 4 July 1994, 9–14. Also appears as pages 135–42 in *Perspectives,* New York: Nation, 1997, and *Taking Liberties: Gay Men's Essays on Politics, Culture, and Sex,* edited by Michael Bronski, 49–60. New York: Richard Kasak, 1996. Kushner writes of the merging of politics and art.

"Some Thoughts about Maria Irene Fornes." In *The Theater of Maria Irene Fornes,* edited by Marc Robinson, 130–33. PAJ Books. Baltimore: Johns Hopkins University Press, 1999.

"The State of the Theatre." *Times Literary Supplement,* 28 April 1995, 14. Kushner contributes an essay, along with other theatrical practitioners, on contemporary theater.

"Stroking at the Easel." *Advocate,* 2 September 1997, 72.

"The Theater of Utopia." *Theater* 26, nos. 1–2 (1995): 9–11. Kushner writes of utopian imagery drawn from history and art.

"Three Screeds from Key West." *Harvard Gay and Lesbian Review* 4 (Spring 1997): 20–23. Kushner writes about playwright-activist Larry Kramer.

"Three Screeds from Key West: For Larry Kramer." In *We Must Love One Another or Die: The Life and Legacies of Larry*

Kramer, edited by Lawrence D. Mass, 191–99. New York: St. Martin's Press, 1997. Kushner lauds the accomplishments of Kramer as a gay rights activist and playwright.

"Tony Kushner vs. Robert Brustein: An Angelic Slugfest." *New Republic,* 14 June 1993, 4–5.

"The 20th Century: Good or Bad." *New York Times Magazine,* 20 September 1998, 76–77.

"University or Trade School?" *New York Times,* 28 June 1993, A17.

"Who's the Victim?" *New Yorker,* 30 January 1995, 11.

"Why We Must Fight." *Stage Directions,* June–July 1997, 7.

"Wings of Desire." *Premiere,* October 1997, 70.

"With a Little Help from My Friends." In *The Best Writing on Writing,* edited by Jack Heffron, 1:20–25. 2 vols. Cincinnati: Story Press, 1994–95. Kushner acknowledges the many individuals who contributed to the making of the *Angels in America* plays; it was first published in the *New York Times.*

Interviews

Barrett, Amy. "The Way We Live Now: Questions for Tony Kushner." *New York Times,* 7 October 2001, sec. 6, 211. Kushner discusses his work and the American scene in the aftermath of 9/11 and as *Homebody/Kabul* opened at the New York Theatre Workshop.

Bernstein, Andrea. "Tony Kushner." *Mother Jones,* July–August 1995, 59, 64. Kushner discusses American political history and his plays.

Jones, Adam Mars. "Tony Kushner." In *Platform Papers No. 2: On "Angels in America,"* edited by Giles Croft, 3–15. London: Royal National Theatre of Great Britain, 1992.

"Liza Gets Another Tony." *OUT,* July–August 1994, 62–64, 144–45. Kushner in conversation with Liza Minnelli.

Lubow, Arthur. "Tony Kushner's Paradise Lost." *New Yorker,* 30 November 1992, 59–64. An interview/essay on Kushner after the London production and before the Broadway version of *Angels in America.*

Marvel, Mark. "A Conversation with Tony Kushner." *Interview* 24 (February 1994): 84. Kushner discusses his work, most particularly *Angels in America*.

Raymond, Gerard. "Q and A with Tony Kushner." *Theatre Week,* 20–26 December 1993, 14–20. Kushner discusses his work, most particularly *Angels in America* on Broadway.

Savran, David. "Tony Kushner." In *The Playwright's Voice: American Dramatists on Memory, Writing and the Politics of Culture,* 87–118. New York: Theatre Communications Group, 1999. Also included in *Speaking on Stage: Interviews with Contemporary American Playwrights*, edited by Philip C. Kolin and Colby H. Kullman, 291–313. Tuscaloosa: University of Alabama Press, 1996, and in abridged form as "Tony Kushner Considers the Longstanding Problems of Virtue and Happiness," *American Theatre,* October 1994, 20–27, 100–104. A wide-ranging interview in which Kushner discusses his work to that point, American theater in general, and the nature of activist drama, as well as influences on his work, personal life, and overall aesthetic principles.

Szentgyorgyi, Tom. "Look Back—and Forward—in Anger." *Theater Week,* 14–20 January 1991, 15–19. An interview with Kushner after the New York production of *A Bright Room Called Day*, as *Angels in America* was rehearsing at the Mark Taper Forum.

Vorlicky, Robert H., ed. *Tony Kushner in Conversation.* Ann Arbor: University of Michigan Press, 1997. An invaluable collection of Kushner essays from the beginning of his playwriting career in the 1980s to 1997, with many wide-ranging essays, as well as some tied directly to a play or production in progress.

Weber, Carl. "I Always Go Back to Brecht." *Brecht Yearbook / Das Brecht-Jahrbuch* 25 (1995): 67–88. A dialogue between Kushner and his graduate school mentor, who introduced him to the plays and theories of Bertolt Brecht.

Selected Works on Tony Kushner

Collections of Essays

Bloom, Harold, ed. *Tony Kushner*. Bloom's Modern Critical Views. New York: Chelsea House, 2005. A collection of previously published critical essays on Kushner's work.

Brask, Per, ed. *Essays on Kushner's Angels*. Winnipeg, Manitoba: Blizzard, 1996. The first collection of critical essays on *Angels in America* focuses on international productions.

Fisher, James, ed. *Tony Kushner: New Essays on the Art and Politics of the Plays*. Jefferson, N.C.: McFarland, 2006. Critical essays on Kushner's major plays and adaptations.

Geis, Deborah R., and Steven F. Kruger, eds. *Approaching the Millennium: Essays on Angels in America*. Ann Arbor: University of Michigan Press, 1997. Scholarly essays responding to diverse aspects of *Angels in America*.

Monographs

Fisher, James. *The Theater of Tony Kushner: Living Past Hope*. New York: Routledge, 2001. Revised 2002. A study of Kushner's major plays, adaptations, one-act plays, and political activism, including previously unpublished works.

Kekki, Lasse. *From Gay to Queer: Gay Male Identity in Selected Fiction by David Leavitt and in Tony Kushner's Play "Angels in America I–II."* New York: Peter Lang, 2003. Emphasizes homosexual aspects of Kushner's *Angels in America* plays.

Critical Essays and Selected Reviews

Blanchard, Bob. "Playwright of Pain and Hope." *Progressive* 58 (October 1994): 42–44. An examination of Kushner as a political dramatist.

Bottoms, Stephen J. "Re-staging Roy: Citizen Cohn and the Search for Xanadu." *Theatre Journal* 48, no. 2 (1996): 157–84. Analyzes the significance of the Roy Cohn character in *Angels in America*.

Brantley, Ben. "A *Dybbuk* Foresees 'The Martyred Dead.'" *New York Times,* 17 November 1997, E5.

———. "How Aged These Sonnets, but They Doth Speak Fresh." *New York Times,* 23 June 1998, E1.

———. "Outsiders Bond in a South of Roiling Change." *New York Times,* 1 December 2003, B1, 5.

Brustein, Robert. "Angels in Afghanistan." *New Republic,* 18 March 2002, 27.

———. "Angles in America." *New Republic,* 24 May 1993, 29–31.

———. "The Great Work Falters." *New Republic,* 27 December 1993, 25–28.

———. "*Slavs!*" *New Republic,* 30 January 1995, 30–31.

Canby, Vincent. "In *Slavs!* Kushner Creates Tragic Burlesque." *New York Times,* 18 December 1994, sec. 2, 5, 24.

———. "Two *Angels,* Two Journeys, in London and New York." *New York Times,* 30 January 1994, 5, 22. An examination of similarities and differences in the productions and audience responses to *Angels in America* on Broadway and in London.

Elkin-Squitieri, Michelle. "'The Great Work Begins': Apocalyptic and Millenarian Vision in *Angels in America.*" *Anglophonia* 3 (1998): 203–12. A critical study of apocalyptic visions in *Angels in America.*

Feingold, Michael. "Bright Words." *Village Voice,* 15 January 1991, 87. A review of *A Bright Room Called Day.*

———. "Spectacle and Spirit." *Village Voice,* 25 November 1997, 111. A review of Kushner's adaptation of *A Dybbuk.*

Felman, Jyl Lynn. "Lost Jewish (Male) Souls: A Midrash on *Angels in America.*" *Tikkun* 10 (May–June 1995): 27–30. A critical examination of Jewish characters in *Angels in America.*

Fisher, James. "'The Angels of Fructification': Tennessee Williams, Tony Kushner, and Images of Homosexuality on the American Stage." *Mississippi Quarterly* 49 (Winter 1995–96): 13–32. A critical comparison of the plays of Tennessee Williams and Kushner set into an overview of the history of gay drama in American theater.

———. "Between Two Worlds: Ansky's *The Dybbuk* and Kushner's *A Dybbuk.*" *Soviet and East European Performance* 18, no. 2

(1998): 20–32. Critically compares early productions of S. Ansky's *The Dybbuk* with Kushner's free adaptation of the play.

———. "Tony Kushner's Metaphorical Jew." In *You Should See Yourself: Jewish Identity in Postmodern American Culture*, edited by Vincent Brook, 76–94. Rutgers, N.J.: Rutgers University Press, 2006. A critical examination of major Jewish characters in Kushner's plays.

———. "Troubling the Waters: Visions of Apocalypse in Wilder's *The Skin of Our Teeth* and Kushner's *Angels in America*." In *Thornton Wilder: New Essays*, edited by Martin Blank, Dalma Hunyadi Brunauer, and David Garrett Izzo, 391–407. West Cornwall, Conn.: Locust Hill Press, 1998. A critical comparison of images of apocalypse in Thornton Wilder's plays and in Kushner's *Angels in America*.

Freedman, Jonathan. "Angels, Monsters, and Jews: Intersections of Queer and Jewish Identity in Kushner's *Angels in America*." *PMLA* 113 (January 1998): 90–102. Kushner's merging of gay and Jewish issues in *Angels in America* is critically examined.

Heilpern, John. "Zounds! Kushner's *Homebody/Kabul* Is Our Best Play in Last 10 Years." *New York Observer*, 5 January 2002, 1. A review of *Homebody/Kabul* in its production at the New York Theatre Workshop.

Hitchens, Christopher. "*Angels* over Broadway." *Vanity Fair*, March 1993, 72–76. An investigative report revealing the difficulties surrounding preparations for *Angels in America* for Broadway.

Klein, Joe. "When Hollywood Gets Terrorism Right." *Time*, 9 January 2006, 21. The political columnist praises *Munich*, along with the films *Paradise Now* and *Syriana* and the television series *24*, for responsibly exploring the moral issues of terrorism.

Kramer, Yale. "Angels on Broadway." *American Spectator* 26 (July 1993): 18–25. An investigative report on backstage struggles in getting *Angels in America* produced on Broadway.

Lahr, John. "After Angels: Tony Kushner's Promethean Itch." *New Yorker*, 3 January 2005, 42–52. A profile of Kushner emphasizing his life and work as he approached fifty.

———. "Angels on Broadway." *New Yorker*, 23 May 1993, 137.

———. "Beyond Nelly." *New Yorker,* 23 November 1992, 126–30. A profile on Kushner and the nature of his theatrical work as *Angels in America* came to Broadway.

———. "Hail, Slavonia." *New Yorker,* 9 January 1995, 85–87.

———. "Underwater Blues: History and Heartbreak in *Caroline, or Change.*" *New Yorker,* 8 December 2003, 122–24.

Lubow, Arthur. "Tony Kushner's Paradise Lost." *New Yorker,* 30 November 1992. An analysis of Kushner's work, particularly in regard to *Angels in America* as it was first produced in New York.

McNulty, Charles. "*Angels in America:* Tony Kushner's Theses on the Philosophy of History." *Modern Drama* 39 (Spring 1996): 84–96. A critical analysis of *Angels in America* in light of theories of history, including those of Walter Benjamin.

Minwalla, Framji. "Tony Kushner's *Homebody/Kabul*: Staging History in a Post-Colonial World." *Theater* 33, no. 1 (2003): 29–43. A critical analysis of *Homebody/Kabul* stressing its historical and political content.

Montgomery, Benilde. "*Angels in America* as Medieval Mystery." *Modern Drama* 44 (Winter 1998): 596–606. A critical reflection on Prior Walter's descent from an historically important family from the Middle Ages in *Angels in America*.

Norden, Edward. "From Schnitzler to Kushner." *Commentary* 99 (January 1995): 51–58. A critical assessment of Kushner in comparison with Arthur Schnitzler and other dramatists exploring eroticism.

Quindlen, Anna. "Happy and Gay." *New York Times,* 6 April 1994, A21. A column in praise of the message of compassion in *Angels in America*.

Quinn, John R. "Corpus Juris Tertium: Redemptive Jurisprudence in *Angels in America*." *Theatre Journal* 48 (1996): 79–90. A critical analysis of the ways in which Kushner depicts the law and the legal profession in *Angels in America*.

Reston, James, Jr. "A Prophet in His Time." *American Theatre*, March 2002, 28–30, 50–53. A long review essay on *Homebody/*

Kabul in its New York Theatre Workshop production and the significance of Kushner's work.

Rich, Frank. "*A Bright Room Called Day*." *New York Times,* 8 January 1990, C11.

———. "'Caroline,' Kennedy and Change." *New York Times,* 7 December 2003, sec. 2, 1, 24.

———. "Embracing All Possibilities in Art and Life." *New York Times,* 5 May 1993, C15–16.

———. "Following an Angel for a Healing Vision of Heaven on Earth." *New York Times,* 24 November 1993, B1, 4.

———. "Making History Repeat, Even against Its Will." *New York Times,* 8 January 1991, C11, 14.

———. "Marching out of the Closet, into History." *New York Times,* 10 November 1992, C15, 22.

———. "The Reaganite Ethos, with Roy Cohn as a Dark Metaphor." *New York Times,* 5 March 1992, C15, 21.

Richards, David. "*Angels in America:* An Epic, All Right, but It's the Details and Future That Count." *New York Times,* 16 May 1993, sec. 2, 1, 7.

———. "History Hung Over: Post-Soviet Aches and Absurdities." *New York Times,* 13 December 1994, C17–18.

———. "Kushner's Adaptation of a French Classic." *New York Times,* 20 January 1994, C15–16.

Rogoff, Gordon. "Angels in America, Devils in the Wings." *Theater* 24, no. 2 (1993): 21–29. An examination of the on- and offstage efforts to get *Angels in America* to Broadway.

Savran, David. "Ambivalence, Utopia, and a Queer Sort of Materialism: How *Angels in America* Reconstructs the Nation." *Theatre Journal* 47 (May 1995): 207–27. A critical examination of the intersections of history, homosexuality, and images of utopia in *Angels in America*.

Smith, Matthew Wilson. "*Angels in America:* A Progressive Apocalypse." *Theater* 29, no. 3 (Fall 1999): 153–65. Critically analyzes the seemingly antithetical notions of progress and apocalypse in *Angels in America*.

Solomon, Alisa. "Review: *The Illusion*." *Village Voice,* 8 November 1988, 100.

————. "Seeking Answers in Yiddish Classics." *New York Times,* 16 November 1997, sec. 2, 7, 22.

Tucker, Scott. "Our Queer World: A Storm Blowing from Paradise." *Humanist* 53 (November–December 1993): 32–35. Drawing on Walter Benjamin's influence on *Angels in America,* this analysis examines progressive notions in the play.

Tuss, Alex J. "Resurrecting Masculine Spirituality in Tony Kushner's *Angels in America*." *Journal of Men's Studies* 5 (August 1996): 49–63. Variant images of masculinity in *Angels in America* are critically analyzed.

Index